CU00660207

JOHN MARTIN

COLLECTED POEMS

VOLUME 10: LANDOR ROAD

Published by Bysshe-Mendel Verlag

bysshemendelverlag@gmail.com

Copyright © John Martin 2016

John Martin asserts his moral right to be identified as the author of this work

ISBN 978-0-9934630-1-3

Printed and bound by Short Run Press Limited, Exeter

All rights reserved. No part of this publication may be reproduced, stored in a retrieval system, or transmitted, in any form or by any means, electronic, mechanical, photocopying, recording or otherwise, without the prior permission of the publishers.

LANDOR ROAD

John Martin

Bysshe-Mendel Verlag

Que sólo de pensar que está olvidado
De su bella pastora con gran pena
Se deja maltratar en tierra ajena
El pecho del amor muy lastimado.

San Juan de la Cruz

For by the violence of their Imaginations, having taken their
Fancies for Realities, they make right deductions from
them...Hence it comes to pass, that a Man, who is very sober, and
of a right Understanding in all other things, may in one particular
be as frantick, as any in Bedlam; if either by any sudden very
strong impression or long fixing his Fancy upon one sort of
Thoughts, incoherent Ideas have been cemented together so
powerfully, as to remain united.

Locke

We speak of friends and their fortunes,
And of what they did and said,
Till the dead alone seem living,
And the living alone seem dead.

And at last we hardly distinguish
Between the ghosts and the guests;
And a mist and shadow of sadness
Steals over our merriest jests.

Longfellow

As courting penguins drop at consorts' feet
pebbles to prove their means, or to impress
shyness that must have tokens of address,
dumbness that must be taken as discreet,

I gather frequent beakfuls to compete
for favours; please consider them no less
that they are polished semi-preciousness,
not even bricks.
                    And do not try to eat.

Hapless this penguin, instinct out of hand,
no-one to woo but still he scours the shore,
his cairns have all but blotted out the sand;

some wave may swoop and carry them away -
against it happen he must pile up more
who thinks these walls will keep the tide at bay.

The pallid wash of dusk hangs thick and blue
on blackened branches dripping over walls,
the loneliness of garden smoke recalls
the fainting memory, through smell, of you.

The fields are chaste,
                                though melancholy snow
melts into colour with the fading light,
the garments of intoxicated night
spread through the shadows with an astral glow.

This pungent recollection in the air
awakens every other dormant sense
until I see and hear you everywhere;

the smoke has blotted out my indigence;
we touch as nightfall glistens on your hair,
and for this moment it seems time relents.

With one sweet tension let our frames explode,
   until it do
   and I drive through
I must sit and scribble till I shed my load
   that is not heavy
   though it levy
taxes that in bees are honey,
the point of yearning fixed upon one goad.

Oh why do time and distance so encage,
   within our loins,
   a miser's coins,
exacting computation of a wage,
   but word for word,
   the bird,
singing of our patrimony
imprisoned in the whiteness of a page.

With one releasing bolt across the sky
   let it nestle,
   you the pestle
pounding and the mortar being ground am I
   in which pieces
   that our peace is
waiting for increased releasing from fly by.

Rippling outwards from this chatter,
waves of sound begin to clutter
silence;
        songs that once could raise a tear,
persistent, distant, bruise the air
amidst the rhythm of this clatter,
blunt the sharpened edge of fear
        to such a drear
        and dull despair
till I at last no longer care.

Stirred from sleeping, old tunes batter
our emotions which then splutter:
fuel to
        waken up a dormant fire,
encumber slumber, and restore
forgotten feelings which now splatter
all the echoes of desire,
        flaming higher;
        although no more,
they burn as brightly as before.

Revenants resume their patter,
find their voices, as they mutter
mouthless,
        rise and fall with each new tide,
controlling rolling, as birds wade.
Sound or silence, does it matter,
feeling is the same inside,
        for those who've died
        and were dismayed
by music, stranded or waylaid.

Former figures firmer, fatter,
stretch their wings and faintly flutter:
feelings

       false and feeble, as they fall,
revolving, solving nothing still
despite the promises that flatter;
the soft echoes of withdrawal
       that faintly call
       your name until
the emptiness has had its fill.

Now the shadows start to stutter,
a crescendo soon to shatter
solace:
       all this dwindles to a new
forgetting, letting all dreams go;
the sudden closing of the shutter
puts all prospect out of view,
       and even you
       pulled in the flow
by this receding water's tow.

That too complacent telephone, a squat,
smug, sated image of felinity
that mauled what flew from me to you to me,
reminds me of a self-sufficient cat

that snoozes in the sun contentedly
and kept the birds at bay and grew so fat,
whose being was qualitative disparate,
haunting the sleepless wainscot silently.

Often I've tried to bell it, for its claws
dig deeper into me than any syringe,
injecting toxic fluid through my pores

that my unclotting blood just goes on gushing.
Ever forestalled, presuming not to impinge,
I give my heart at last to be her cushion.

DIAMOND FOUNDLING

Glass-baby, is that sparkle crying?
We cut your eyes to irrigate
    our desert with glass tears.
You cannot live because you are not dying.
Oh shut your porthole eyes
    my diamond child.
You're always lying.

Oh foundling child if you don't hush your noise
we'll have to smash you like a china pig
    and out will tumble all we've saved for you
which we shall give away to proper boys
who aren't afraid to break
    a diamond child
in bits like all their toys.

Our little precious, jewels are such a treasure:
we pack you up in cotton wool
    for ransom.You are fragile.
You were minded to give all others pleasure -
they reflect themselves in you,
    sweet diamond child,
and learn to measure.

We rock you in a cradle made of gold -
what need to smile when you are faceted
    in shrieks of blue that sting a kiss from light?
You can't be young because you can't be old.
So give us real value
    diamond child
when you are sold.

Crystal-infant, please avoid a scandal,
assaulting air with coloured knives

7

you've sharpened on your eyes.
You have become too burning cold to handle,
dagger drowned in your own depth of tears,
    you, diamond child,
are just a seen-through vandal.

Symbolic swans have no feet, nor is lust
like candles, but white memorised desire
can perish, as the moth upon the fire,
and fumbling schoolboys find a rhyme in trust,
for yearning burns, but then returns to dust.
The body is a bubble we require
(yet are platonic, therefore aiming higher)
the baser instinct in us is nonplussed.

I was – the bubble pricked, and blew again;
love is, as Shelley wrote, transcendent power
directing (tropically) a weather-vane;
for lesser poets, though, the briefest flower,
or frost collecting on the window-pane,
or wolf that waits in patience to devour,
with extra limb (like this) to pace the anxious hour.

He asked who owned the island, set his heart
on buying it, and got it for a song;
he swam across one evening to re-start
his life, which had gone wrong.

A barren rock that he would cultivate
and make a second paradise;
but only tourists came to speculate
and say how very nice.

MAKE-BELIEVE

That child in mother's shoes too big for it
affects no limping as she slurs her feet;
she trails a handbag filled with coloured stones
and an old lip-stick, all packed neat;
she'll come to look for it when playing's done
    as if she had begun
what matters.

The more she whimpers more she clutches at
the indignant doll she squeezes into life;
she prinks the lashes, she can make it cry
or close its eyes, she is a wife;
she'll come to succour it when playing's done
    as if she had begun
what matters.

Grown-ups look on to watch their children learn
passions and incidences to restrain;
when all were young we played the grooming game
exploring areas of pain;
soon we must break to them that playing's done
    because they have begun
what matters.

CROSS PURPOSES

Where shall I look? Your parents have compiled
these albums; on the persons, not the view,
I linger - to identify the child
that strained its eager smiling, became you.

I cannot read there any more than since
I have been able to unlock your eyes;
you had to crush the darling of these prints
for rougher circumstance to catechise.

Can cameras lie, that froze you in this trance,
or did it freeze you once and you're still cold?
I cannot say it told you in advance

how time would scar, not features, with its file,
but an imagination, for, grown old,
you've brought your head with you, but not your smile.

An hour or more I've watched you auscultate
his heart complaint - you've wrestled to release
a melancholy bird in you - palpate
more gently, I feel sorry for the keys,

which have my sympathy, for he is sick
with all that yearning. Tell me why you strive
with passionate, precise arithmetic
to keep a patient moribund alive.

Oh then I saw your eyes, how they pursue
interminable langours in some mist
that webs you from me when I try to woo.

You seldom speak, therefore I learn to hear

what voice I can, and try to get the gist:
your look so sensitive, your hands severe.

You call it true to answer, no, to *is
that black*, when it is white, or we can't name
the colour. Therefore your analysis,
you say, can't lie. Must I obey your game's

impassioned, so-called scientific rules
because you ask the questions? I deny
that everything consists of molecules,
by saying what is true can also lie?

Why does such certainty excite your pulse
if you are right? Do you sniff out some treason
because I say that not to lie is false?

You have been blinkered in your borrowed sight,
a principle of insufficient reason:
could I be wrong to you, and yet be right?

I must be careful here or I may tread
upon some mine implanted in your brain;
to forgive can be a sort of hatred
and detonate another sort of pain.

Yes, yes, indeed, I have a poet's knack
to monger words not saying what they mean,
all that I've said, to please you, I'll take back, -
I only tried to keep my diction clean.

What shall we talk about now you have won, -
I'm sorry, now that truth prevailed? I still
believe your spectacles put out the sun
but proving it would have to make you blind:

12

the care that holds my temper whispers: *kill!*
for it is cruelty to be so kind.

I have a way of thinking, not quite straight,
I know, don't speak, but rather catch my breath
in wonder at what's lost to expiate
my mispronouncing lisp, your shibboleth.

You think I am attacking your belief -
susceptible of doubt, can they be facts?
Tone-deaf to harmony that succours grief
my discipline from dissonance extracts.

Likewise your arrogating terms preserve
structure, co-ordination, measurement,
a mantle that illuminates the nerve...

thus run our secret searchings parallel,
where either breaks the other's filament,
which we had laid to lead us out of hell.

Distance between us is what brings us close,
the very appetite that would destroy
that acrimony makes you bellicose:
the rancour of a child, because his toy

is faithful to its nature, not to him,
will teach, when he has broken it, respect;
if he lets water win, he'll learn to swim.
To honour you, you force me to reject

your inner principle: if I embraced
your outlook I would cut you dead! How mend
may we each other, then, unless disgraced
of what each is himself? I come disguised

into your camp at night - let us suspend
hostilities: but am not recognised.

We are too constant. Human faithlessness
is wishful thinking. Only when we chafe
at bondage know ourselves. How much the less
possess another whom our loving strafe;

dog-fights and high conceit! Reasons of state
eschew this compromise, may dabble here,
when all else fails a policy of hate
may be pursued to wake us out of fear.

We will keep faith! We have made common cause
with our investment, we will not betray!
Some indiscretions issuing in wars

have put the people's freedom into play.
They wanted healing water that restores,
but seeing the Jordan muddy, turned away.

Wrangling had jabbed him early from the womb
embittered creasing made mercurial
in sanction; quick-bitten fingernails exhume
blood-angled lips of snug marsupial,

had fainted from her kisses, à la French;
he lost his tongue, the bit between his teeth,
her shocked lubricity ran through the trench,
each lost his head, blast-withered to a wreath.

Loth wrung-neck chicken to relinquish pride
shimmies a bright perception, coats its wings,
to be an angel, in thalidomide,
dances on needles; from the head they lop,

a quantum speculation's augurings
identify the message in its crop.

Relentless standstill, comes this python on
like mother, fancy at first sight, in coils
of welcome, bowing; black, confederate swan
that numbs the graspless air with healing oils

of intimacy: white rat is amazed
to ease response with this rigidity
of knowing look bewilderment has dazed
in bristling terror at such quiddity.

Special indifference has marked him out
to be devoured where the mind can sprawl
in dreamless indolence beyond all doubt;

soundless surrendering, the drowned will soothe
these recognitions from a washed eyeball:
grateful release all round. The function smooth.

We need a language purged of all device,
that might lick silence like a tongue of smoke
discharged from fervour, some stone-dry qui tollis
that each should understand when any spoke.

It should reach heaven, like a new-found word,
no etymology, but quite undressed,
perfect and elemental like a bird,
intact and broken, both, like bread that's blessed,

and without subsidy - the language greys
from too much scrubbing to uncover truth;
the best to strive for honestly obeys
provisional compunction, playing games,

that smoothes the possible with civil oath,
denoting what promotes our unheard screams.

Words played against each other shine and rub
out individual obscurity:
what life-denying wounds may language swab
that is discoloured by impurity;

for it means nothing till it come to ears
that take instruction, settle, plot a course;
the granite that we strain after to pierce
may lend inclemency itself, remorse

just deafens it or else it echoes back
its answer by default of substances:
well, that's what comes of talking to the rock.

There must be other ways to speak than tongues
that twist about this penitential maze,
ascend to heaven on horizontal rungs.

There is no means to take away the cup
we pray into to give beseeching form;
some say the stones in anguish should rise up
to keep all bleeding children out of harm;

what vanity - have you heard stones respond
to terror? Seen them soak up blood? The claps
of thunder in syllabics wave a wand
that cracks the stone, but would you kiss such lips?

They may not be corrupted into voice,
or we'd be crushed beneath their eloquence
of uncommiseration at our loss;

they trap no weepings where the mourned are fumbled
after, suppressing echoes of events
that we break open, hallowed, hollowed, humbled.

Rain in the gardens,
and the sun my ring on her finger.

Have in the pale raining yourself veiled,
have in the grey waning hidden, that your eyes
would blind me, cat of the mountain,
scrawny reachless whither make I steps.
For in the darkness heavy with your blood
two eyes are peering, that cannot be seen,
unless my turning on them fluoresce
the arrows of the forest drenched in flame
upon the target moon to shoot their aim.

Green light, lady-luminous-eyes-lidded
till I know where I am not going, know enough
to cross that forest where corpses crawl
for the lifeless stamp of dead hands,

then, to where your eyes are pulsing,
green-cold-fire that does not consume.

Behind these curtains blindness weaves with pain
I see you dancing in the torches' power.
I know you are a million miles away
upon the shadowed and conceptive moon,
and move in bloodless motion.
                              I am worn and thin.

But I will come to find you out,
shall walk, shall wake, shall woo, and then shall win.

You are as far, and further, from me now
as that horizon
where I look all evening:
all my feeling focused
as eyes widen into meaning without speech.

I could reach
some understanding,
as these hidden birds are singing
and these waters lip the beach.

Like a boat with hardened timbers,
shipping water, always leaking, barely floating,
till I look towards the mountains
to project this useless yearning,
knowing that you are not returning,
saw the hump of dwindling ridges,
grave liquidity of elephants
in procession, like my wants,
pursuing streams from memory.

All this clamour of my needing
trample could me underfoot.

Wild the flowing, gentle greyness
fuses rapture of postponing,
our atoning,
stately through the clouds proceeding
(telephoning, interceding)
not restoring here below,
in that elephantine swaying
tusks of snow almost gored me,
nothing softens, no allaying,
but the clarity of snow.

Words come between us,
to whomever we speak,
like buffers - the wordless copulation
has a buffer-function too,
against so sharp a crushing sense
of our impenetrable isolation,
indigence - the jolt is fun,
the truth, not being absolute,
variations on a pun.

Silence is golden,
but it backs a forgeable currency,
liable to inflation.
Which having been said one makes palpable
the isolation with words,
or the scream or the grunt of release,
whoosh, from the accelerator prostate
along the highways of fulfillment,
to what destination...?

No, we do but travel, it is to the roads
we belong, not homes,
nomads we of the lost absolute,
pickers-up of the dropped stitches of time,
parsers of experience's almost untranslatable
clauses.
          From which some may infer that the route
to truth is wordless, others go on talking
to themselves in a mirror.

I just go on calling my half-lies true,
never quite able wholly to mistrust
those that know so much better than I
how to evade the truth of a lie.

This spatchcock broiler, batch of pluck in love;
I wear across my chest a pinchbeck brooch
that touch unvalues; an unleavened loaf
whose gilt assays the sanctifying breach.

Tinker of promises goes spitting pips
of bitterness to count what he can cadge,
to squeeze a thawing from congested pipes,
a ribbing pigeons in his rattled cage.

You get the message! Streaming through the sieve
come muddied waters, semen veined with blood,
a gaze of crystal broken to deceive.

Shall we take notice that we find no heart
in this haruspication fingers bleed;
the fallen shadow stains, portending hurt.

ON THE RETURN OF A FRIEND

Some that enter the room break ice,
like rain come greyly others
that strain not to be dumb
and wash the walls with their long faces,
are pent up into shadows along corners,
are stretched into windows of paleness
onto far perspectives,
                              whose lines
meeting like strings in the piano
converge on stricken wings, -

have we not heard them beat against horizons?

I have found sleep only,
that has rubbed brass from death,
to have erased outrage from faces -

I, far from modest ghost,
slouch a tight-rope of dead self,
have wrapped up the sorrowing net of safety,
return to poke through the past
for a lost vesture -
                              whose great fear,
hope,
        whose love alone a desire to suffer.

Little I still know of you, though fearless,
not quite blind, I knew you, yet no less
a friend that you do not calculate, as I,
the degree to which one may flatter,
to which one may determine
the specific gravity of love-in-friendship.

I would pay no compliment,

the more because you would not fail,
being without guile,
to trust me,
        I could well forget
one rush of solace in the next rejoinder -
yet -
     you entered with the corn-sheaf radiance
of yourself
        no hail embittered and no frost made harsh;
all that you were became a form
to hold yourself -
        as those that shuffle notes
or words or pigment strive for,
whose best wonder is illumination
of duplicity, which this may prove.

I say you entered with effects of love,
as when I say the dew distills upon a curling lip
of blossom, falling from itself,

I say you entered as you are,
held for an instant in a poise
neither the future nor the past will mar.

KLEIN'S CHOICE

To die not suddenly but over years
of slow recession as a surgeon's ward,
to swallow every day the self-same sword,
fed flowers in the saline grail
the brain has withered like a rose
the brain extruded through the nose
is picked upon a fingernail.

With fish-hook eyes
each picks each other up
and bites into the groove of other music,
stoned on soap bubbles
rubbed from a rubber body
erasing itself down quaint horizons of moonlight,
into perspectives of disintegration.
Waking to carbon-copy mornings,
rubber-stamped, constraint of debt -
my heart is mortgaged: I have raised a loan
on it, erased alone by seizure or arrest,
a wrest more gauged to plumb the broken harp.

The grass is sun-scrofulous
the day flakes like old plaster
flesh hangs in grey dewlaps
of leprous alabaster.

The last shreds of mist
hang on a thorn,
sex is the spine
on which love is born.

Against the eclipse
I can only put smoked glass, metaphor,
mixed words monochrome,

then shuffle and reshuffle the restricted sheaf
and organise with paper clips
that order things like kissing lips
into my advocate's brief -
the fractured sun
haranguing an empty court in an action to recover
the certainty of being someone's lover.

If you would know yourself
go not alone,
for solitude breeds only fantasies
of such a self as such a self would please:
despite yourself
the way that you have grown:
and what you hate to be
loving makes known.

From all this there had to be some principle
of cohesion, a commensurate vineyard
of delicate vintage, bodies for bottles,
spiritual slops in frayed skins.

It is a deliberate choice
between chaos and coherence,
to lay us down in the nitrate bath
of the underground assignation,
amongst a people of spectres, ghosts of blood,
worming the entrails of night,
the prescription and accrual of experience
and above all the words like burrs.

Precedents confirm the distinction:
nature's calligraphy has grammar,
for recommending appetite to us,
its minions, enslaves the will,
to tread the inner pattern of the mill,
driven on the whetstone of concupiscence,

delivered blunt; spring withers flowers,
not the other seasons;

                               also has syntax,
once it is spoken, love's tongue
is lax, nature's code broken
published as facts:
nature and love, we thus agreed,
are similar languages
masking our need -
we need each other, together we speak
each a dead language,
poetry and Greek.

LANDOR ROAD

Wasted by selfless waiting in debauch
of deprivation was the consequence
for being constant to one bright, fixed sense
of inner focus then. What quenched the torch,
that led me to the vault, upon the porch
of union and growth? I said, dispense
with having. Strength of you made indigence
a dazzling light, against the darker scorch
of loss. The brand burnt on to make me blind
to what the cave illumined where I hid;
being by you eyeless I could never find
more than the obduracy of the lid
to prove a coffin for you of my mind:
to keep, first give. I didn't and I did.

Now I must leave you to descend alone
the stairs that take me to confront the face
I have been hiding from, my deep disgrace
at holding you, my failure to atone.
What will my head have: flesh, eyes, skin and bone
like any human, such that you can trace
again some slight attraction? Is this place
I'm going a warmer tomb than I have known?
No one can answer - it was built for me
to find a self I never found before;
the lock will yield, but only to one key
(you have) by losing all till I explore
the roots of my despair. Then I shall see
how rich I am in loss, in love how poor.

Because I know past doubt I am not such
as you can love except by standing off,

as I have done and now, however rough
to me, must do again, the tender touch
of your white body has become a crutch
for an old cripple at whom children scoff,
walking with that white rod towards the trough
of dawnless midnight. That is why I clutch,
forgive me, as a drowning man a straw
at everything you offer, having had,
till you, nothing to blunt destruction's claw
except my feelings. Better to be mad,
to see no reason, speechless. What I saw
was double figures even I can add.

What shall I find when I have crossed the rift
between me and my nature, past deceit,
in this first triumph, ultimate defeat
of run-proof monochrome, my final gift,
which is to offer up myself in shrift
of cherished secrets? I shall be complete,
shall need no longer, selfhood then replete,
to smother you with shiftless, sinking drift
of agony, in which the antidote
for an addiction is the drug. I choose
the essence of the petal, not its coat
of transient lushness: that I mean to lose
to anyone. It's yours, not mine. Remote
reciprocation, this, the who, not whose.

Even a fool like me knows that was brave,
false magnanimity, an utter lie -
of course my love would not, but I would, die,
your eyes on someone else would be my grave -
so why be pompous when I ought to rave;
if I don't trust you, you will follow sly
concealing glances - why should you deny -

to take to faces is not to deprave.
We are not skin-deep lovers, born of charm, -
how could you think that since my face is flat?
If you like faces, fondling, what's the harm -
it is your pleasure, we are disparate.
So pick the fruits, I'll do my best to farm
my shrubless rock, nor wonder what you're at.

There is intention and there is the scream
that rises daily in my strangled throat
at certain meanings. They are not remote,
although I see they must appear extreme.
Shut out, I know, I must the golden dream,
abandon towers, empty out the moat -
there is no constancy in man or goat
if either's instinct press for wombs to teem.
How can I bring myself to terms with this -
you like a body, any, to embrace;
no doubt you are not sick to think a kiss
would be reciprocated from the face
you look at. I to my analysis
to cure me: you towards your sort of grace.

This is the second instance I renounce
holding what made the image in my hands,
knowing relinquished having understands
little of why such having's out of bounds.
Now I am one of those face-painted clowns
that take their jitters into foreign lands,
turned upside down to show time-telling sands
run, but being tongueless exiles, gurgle sounds.
You will be spared the sight of such charade
because to see my face expressionless
would not compare at all with the parade
of fanciful excitement you undress.

Your eyes must meet what other eyes displayed,
whilst mine go blank, containing their distress.

That was unworthy - you must feast your fill
on instinct's summons: opposite of pain
is alien beauty's fertilising rain
on your parched desert. If you feel the thrill
of grace in bodies why should I be ill
because my body's not the only drain
of coursing loin-ache? Why should you abstain
from pleasure such as groins not mine distil?
I am no statue of the form your eyes
will follow, rather what is here inside,
not palpable, but abstract properties
enliven in you - otherwise it's pride
that makes me wish entire being ties
you to me. Body not, but that your bride.

Dreams may well shiver but the world looks grey
I open eyes upon when turning back
against the spectres that made my world black
with grasping shadows melting at the day.
Why, on the threshold, barring me the way
to seeing clearly, till my dreaming crack,
these ghosts were summoned, pointing out a track
to dwindling definition, I can't say.
Wise men will guide me now to love without
the need for any but an abstract friend -
I can be proud in this: yet in a drought
who harvests flowers from the long-feared end
of withered love, for nothing here will sprout;
I hoped for fruit, but even so I'll tend.

Twice is enough of farming the drear, vast

and sterile acres, hoping to perfect
in a caress my inner self's defect
of wholeness - all you are will last
my life ahead, that is, my life that's past.
So call me self-sufficient and direct
your gaze where that in you will grow erect
and blossom for you. Twice I am aghast
at the phenomenal impermanence
of what the focus fixes on, to turn
and turn again away from me. My sense
must live its crippledness, but I can burn
from fire that is not in immanence,
yet what is it I know yet cannot learn?

What am I doing then, to let this urge
graft single pleasure to a double trunk;
or skin-dive only to whatever's sunk
beyond retrieval, drowning in the surge?
What should become of each if each should merge
himself to each so deeply he'd be drunk
like me on death-wish? No! I'll be a monk
again of an abstraction, let that purge
pain if I too much press upon your nerves
or give you pause to question my intent
in touching you, the cavities, the curves;
I'll be platonic, feed off discontent
in solitary worship – if this serves
your wishes, let me shrive and start my lent.

I should write this in blood, for little else
of me remains and semen is an ink
that dries invisibly, and neither's drink
for the dropped-pebble voice still plumbing wells
for water, when it seems my hand misspells
that latter liquid. I have seen you wink

at what you fancy; I have watched the brink
before me beckon, saying this dispels
me through my body to a roomless peace,
the meeting parallels of no more me
because I can't afford to pay the lease
of where we lived together. You'll be free
to squander appetite in warm release;
whilst I'll stop blaming you, that is, not be.

How can I love you, by self-hate consumed?
Why this loathing? Surely I resemble
all those bodies that have made you tremble,
as any would, which in the darkness loomed
as possible. For what have I been groomed
by fingers, my lying down preamble,
deftly probing me to reassemble
a real person. Too much was assumed.
I am not real, I am discarded hopes,
I am the mirror of an image killed
by unpossession. Someone else's gropes
picked clean from limbs what essences had spilled -
let others wash your bed with those sweet soaps,
let others harvest. It was I that tilled.

What do they think I am, to give advice
on being mature? For I am no more whole
that trees have foliage when crushed to coal
beneath the voiceless weight of centuries.
I was prepared to pay this forfeit price,
my own extinction, being the blackened fuel
of other fires, groping like a mole
for light. It seems I have to do it twice.
I'll let them trace the fossil that was leaf,
the skeleton of self I gave to you;
you are the blossom from my graft of grief -

I withered off on purpose, that you grew
to your own stature. Light I saw was brief
and blinded me. Yet what I saw was true.

Am I ungenerous, that can't accept
I am not everything to you because
you're not obsessed; is this sufficient cause
for wanting death, seeing you may have slept,
may sleep again, with anyone? I kept
that part of me for you, although I was
in love with what should give both ore and dross,
and if the ore was mine what wounding wept
in every part of me when you first spoke
upon these trivial mechanics which
made loving possible? Whatever broke
inside me then impoverished the rich
desires. Surely not the shell, the yolk
is loving. Light the power, not its switch?

Images fail me to conceive a frame
to hold your vision with, the sting of tears
makes it too bitter, thinking of the years
you were imprisoned in such blunt self-blame
for being more than mortal, being flame -
the blue, bright core that dresses what it fears
in golden conflagration, flesh that sears
my sensual eloquence until it's tame.
But nothing withered of the inner heat,
as brilliant as a sapphire set in gold,
the blue extravagance, each time we meet,
makes you one secret that could not be told -
but if my lips were forced I'd just repeat:
it does not change - it is the world gets old.

Loins are a tomb where only worms can feed
far off from fingers of the sun that lick
our strivings dry; the sun is not ascetic,
rather like a smile it ripens seed
in barren souls, like mine, that though they bleed
can have no healing from what makes them sick,
that burn like candles would without a wick
or smelling flowers that have turned to weed.
Brief luxury, the swelling radiance
of etiolated petals crushed to spill
the fructifying juice in innocence -
but press them under tomes to dry, you kill
laughter and raise a wraith no wrath relents
whatever you repress to re-distil.

What strangles love in both of us is grief
which is a counterfeit, dissimulates
like a chameleon watching, silent, waits,
and borrows colour from deciduous leaf,
and this because to hide is some relief
if you are hunted. Pain eliminates
some rigour, says the lover, but he hates
the thing that hurts him, giving to a thief.
Deeper, I think, than need and this remorse
that pales full-blooded hunger in desire,
is to turn round on it and feel the force
of all this conflict, yet still to aspire
to reach the unseen, accepting the divorce
implicit in such love, the burn from fire.

What self is dimly slipping from my grasp
that I have clutched at, knowing it was false,
that is sweet melody without a voice,
soft-spoken love that filed me like a rasp,
and stung my skin too often like a wasp:

I stand to live again or die by choice,
where either possibility destroys
all that I am not in one final gasp
of incredulity that you made clear
by coldness, cruelty and indifference;
you will, because you want to, without fear
seduce another for a shambles sense,
whether affection or the sadist's spear,
it all boils down to unremembered grunts.

The grunt of satisfaction still afflicts
the quiet echoing of my dark grave,
where you have bound me, like a worthless slave
of my own nature, for unknown delicts,
within an endless coiling that constricts
all movement. Now commanded to be brave,
I wait for total darkness that will save
my eyes from seeing how desire restricts
itself to willing an extension mind
conceives, and then suppressing by control
and power till the other is quite blind
of self, extinguished, never to be whole,
that having killed my self, you can be kind,
whose pleasure comes from hurting, to console.

What in my person so outrages you?
Why do you hate me, is it for the pain
you know you want to cause me, to restrain
feeling yourself so vulnerable too.
Sure, you would like to offer me a true
affection and intensity - disdain
has masqueraded as desire again,
I am a something lost that you once knew.
It is not love, although you would deny
wanting me harmed, it is from this you hide -

there is ambivalence although you try
to put it from your mind. When I have cried
you felt the glow of warmth, and when I sigh,
you smile with pleasure, knowing you have lied.

I can no longer hide from your deep split
of feeling fond at times of me, intense
but only so by the ambivalence
of need and cruelty, wanting derelict
emotions to be radiantly lit
by a sadistic squashing of my sense
of person, giving me your indigence
of passion, punishing my self for it,
because you cannot face this one deceit:
you wanted to give passion, tenderness
and love to me, but every way you cheat
the root of your concern, my own distress
that feeds destruction in you, incomplete
without an object to endure this mess.

More gentle than I feared was letting go
of what sustained me, unless this is shock
at separation, grief as hard as rock
concussing me till I no longer know
meaning in time at all but this one, slow
residuum of shattered self, a clock
whose limbs death held in momentary lock,
my sort of ever, that can never grow.
Even as I embraced last night's aloof
exclusion, lying separate, I blessed
your new found freedom, thinking this be love,
to give you up beyond what has distressed,
to offer you to others, as a proof
that your first good may be my second best.
That's it. The bond is severed. I have cut

the threads from which we wove togetherness;
all you need take from me is that I bless
you in some hands, not mine; may they rebut
no part of you, nor you of them. The rut
I held you in releases you - no less -
from every vow. May you find that recess
of inner fragrance blossoms, not to shut.
As I must not enquire how you fare
so you are free to banish me. I go
alone again, still shielded by despair,
I wish were total. Even what you owe
have back, yourself made whole, me nothing; where
I've given you. Let neither of each know.

Everyone says - why stress so much the hands
he'll take to succour him when he's alone,
or even kisses, fondlings, or the prone
excitement of delight, controlled by glands.
You seldom mention, say they, why each stands
in such peculiar need beyond the bone
that we're all built on. Now you would disown
emotion's primacy for these slight strands
of nature. I reply: *I have one source,*
a single, strong, entire gush or spring
of passion, focusing on him; divorce
of sex and sentiment would never bring
my certain, glowing self more than remorse -
revoke a part, and that's more damaging.

Follows retort - proud and intolerant,
that can't forgive a natural, warm bias,
only a part of what you love. The liars!
The fuel that friction has made radiant
must burn right out - if I am petulant
then blame this logic: feeling is device

to warm our separation; flames may rise
from burning till both fuel and flame are spent.
Exact! I am put out in him, he said:
my logic says that what he needs is fuel -
it would for me if what I felt were dead
for him. By trying to spark him I am cruel,
for he needs matches from another bed.
For my part I shall never cease to boil
my blood for him, without it's being bled.

How am I so secure in such a boast,
never to smudge my flesh with new perfume?
Is he not second entrant to my tomb,
and leaves it now because he met the ghost
of its first lover's consecrated host
time had not melted. How could there be room
for subsequent ideals in the womb
destroyed by giving birth to what was lost?
You misconceive the destiny: the first
was out of reach and chaste: a fantasy.
What I thought highest was in fact the worst,
what you thought second was love's primacy.
I'll spell it for you: my ideal rehearsed
this cancelling, and this apostasy.

Don't mourn for me- a tickle in the eye
for seven years in subsequent exile
then blinded me, from old corruption's smile;
but seeing nothing, saw no way to die,
yes, seven years remembering not to cry,
I was quite safe, immured upon the isle
of a delusion. Well, I did resile,
this time no irritation but an I
exploding right into the limbs of pain:
credulity; then sight; now self occludes

this separation, but I shall again
be safe enough for where no selfhood broods
upon its loss there's nothing to restrain
the deep extinction this real wound forebodes.

A voice pursues me as I twist and turn
within compunction echoed through a deep
defile of ocean; waking or asleep
I hear it tremble and I have to learn
its lamentable melody, to burn
all substance from your shadow till I reap
the only fruit of you that I can keep
for ever - ashes in a golden urn.
Let them be scattered, even by my arm
that grasps the air to find your falling tone
of inner thirst. I read upon my palm
a senseless tale of love as broken stone
in spirit, not the body I embalm,
which stills the chanting voice to one last groan.

All onlookers that see the trap I'm in
and see so clearly how I can get out,
advise that I'll recover self without
your constant presence that has worn me thin
by our abrasion. Flung away, I spin
from all fixed objects, driven by one doubt;
the echo of one name that I still shout
expands to fill no where where selves begin.
For I must judge the justice of my claim
upon your abstinence, beyond mere need -
the universal echo of your name
reverberates through chambers of my greed -
first principles project a single aim,
not where we rest at all, but when we speed.
To be alone, not have you mediate

between the naked terror and the stroke
of an expression, language's dark cloak
of passed-on meanings, words like love, and fate,
whose mutual definition is to state
the former valued if the last revoke
it, so by broken bonds; in ruins we poke,
each substancing the other, but too late.
Without this mutuality each past
will gorge on speculation, to fulfil
unfinished sentences; a drying ghost
will squeeze glass-eyes because it had to kill
an incompletion, wanting it to last,
but find no way to mend what such eyes spill.

You say you have to run from my despair,
that I was once a better part of you,
but am no longer. I concede this true -
I am absorbed, for you have stripped me bare
of old illusions. Now you cannot dare
to be unhappy, lacking courage too,
to hope beyond experience's few
securities. You are worn down with care
and I am burdensome. You must be free
of my great shadow lengthening to brood
upon your future. Absence will decree
its sort of shadow; its peculiar food
that never satisfies. So, leaving me,
you'll take the promise out of being lewd.

We are controlled by forces that destroy
the very object that they seek to build;
almost like victims, now, but yet who willed
themselves their own destruction. Wanting joy,
we found that everything we touched would cloy
the appetite that fostered it; this killed

desire; we disguised the pain of guilt
as love's intensity, then broke the toy.
Locked in the struggle not to suffer pain,
we cannot face the consequence of choice,
which is for each to suffer self again
unhidden in a reassuring voice,
without all confirmation; break the chain
that binds us to a self that self-destroys.

Last evening's dying sky a passage-bird
of whom my mind the cage; presaging snows
on bleak escarpments, I must now disclose
that prisoner, nor fetter it with word
to wound directly, or the sighed, unheard
reproach of this betrayal. In the throes
of unkept faith, my faith is kept and grows
each day upon the very loss it feared.
These intuitions prove my trust acute
that I could over-ride them. I condemn
no part of your disloyalty. I dispute
no claim on you for others; master them
I cannot; broken cup from bleeding root
it was. It spilled. Hurt. Healed. I am the stem.

A broken faith has this strange property:
it is a bud that breaks, that blossoms white,
that aches the air with presages of night
and burdens it with yearning, like a tree
that's scarred by flushing into mystery;
a trust let drop, I promise, will not blight
the land it falls on, but the dim grows bright
from it. Nothing you've ever done robs me
because I give it back to you, your soul,
or call it seed of self beneath the green,
the one true lasting, broken to be whole

in anguished fusing of ideal and been,
the so-called ineradicable goal
of guiltless love. Forget what comes between,

Since souls are substanceless without the name,
or limb, of pleasure whence we suck its sweet
or melancholy juices, obsolete
by definition in the sexual game,
how am I certain we are still the same
but better, now another is replete
with this your shadow. I cannot compete
with what is over. No - it is a flame -
it might have tickled both, or warmed the skin;
for you it might have blustered to a glow
on dusty embers, spectrally and thin,
consuming either; as the clock-hands go
across blank faces in that union:
I take the inner pulse. That's all I know.

You kept the secret that you had not kept
our secret solitude, but made a breach
with some stray body coming within reach,
and could not sleep at all because you slept
at random, weep, because your body wept
whose tears I dry on mine; lay with a leach
of pleasure masking guilt that would impeach
your inner person. Every way you stepped
in treachery until the words grew fierce
with murder and you dropped that burden - spoke
of your destruction, knowing it would pierce
through me; and so it did. But nothing broke
except my loneliness in your remorse
which shared turned all that screeching to a croak.

I am not worthy to forgive; I can

say nothing changes that I see in you,
but I'm your equal only, as untrue
as any human: take this gift - such pain
as this has caused me earns alone disdain
from my real vision. Nothing I could do
would alter what is over. Yet I knew,
without your telling, you would break this chain -
I was ready. Not for me, absolving,
but for you to take me back as what I
am for you. Myself, I have been passing
often over this unreal boundary
of dispossession. What you did will sting
despite intention. I must let it be.

All sun today I've run familiar halls
of broken selfhood, not because I lost
our one fused isolatedness but lest
it never was; these hardened, flexing hells
perform a penance in the search for wholes
in one another that this guise may last
beyond dissembling, or what hate released
to shed the pressure, that such rupture heals.
I'm talking, thinking, running for my life
which I count nothing now except that torn
it would deliver you beyond relief
to your rough devil, to perfect his tune
of your destruction. Let me live for love
as I am dying for need, that that atone.

I took your dream to heart: reckless you sped
in hurtling break-neck haste, through a miasm
of urgent noxiousness, a gravel chasm
the car could hardly hold. The stranger's bed.
Disaster to avert, to find me dead,
or that in you that sweetens, not the spasm

or sting of degradation in orgasm,
you spun towards two bee-hives in your head,
which you called me, because you could have hurt
with all that power and wiped out utterly
their golden freshness, crushed into the dirt.
Your dream was prescient in mystery
if you will heed it, driving more alert,
and see what comes of infidelity.

Loving is bee-hives: surely it won't sting:
therefore that image, was it love or hate
you almost flattened by precipitate
compulsion, to spit away the honeying
enrichment, or to howl instead of sing?
Why were there two you could annihilate
and saw this only when almost too late
you were upon them in your ravening?
You know your dreaming, what it signifies
of inner motive, conflict or regret -
therefore your dreams issue in anguished cries
that wake me often, though I seldom get
much meaning from them. Now I see that lies
harvest my honey in their strangling net.

It failed, that first attempt to reunite
lost halves of self: the flesh rejects such graft,
the senses gleam as blade to body's haft;
we stitch up touchy skins with threads of spite.
The strands of tenderness that waves may knit
with shuttling kisses tugging at the weft
between the warp may leave the palate cleft,
that when we try to speak we merely spit.
If words prove carriers of a disease
that breeds in drains, why should we crush the host
to death with fingers which although they squeeze

define most sweetly with their lightest touch?
For either way a clean affection's lost,
whose weakness is the strength with which it clutch.

We're treading into darkness, towards dawn
tonight, to sleep alone without what gave
occasional solidity. We'll crave
each other's nakedness that we have worn
through fear of being naked, being born
completely: womb for lovers is a grave
and love a stranglehold, unless we save
each real self by learning how to mourn
the loss of crutches, false intensity,
the prison that my greediness conspired
to shut you in. Now I have set you free -
to guard your wholeness, beyond what required;
confirmation your everything is me:
I love much more in you than I desired,

Too simple now to say we could be friends,
and but for my desire to possess
we might have been and given tenderness
where it was needed. Let me make amends,
not by returning, for that purpose ends
with this beginning, not under duress
of pale enslavement - that our friendship bless
two growing wholer. Will it? That depends.
On whether we can mean the words we speak
and have a conversation without lies:
but better to say nothing than be meek
in false compliance. If you never phone
I'll take it I have withered in your eyes
and nothing I could do now would atone.

Of your blue body time will wash its hands
like soap, that I watch over tenderly
tonight. When, I shall give my sanity
gladly, to scrawling cancelled ampersands
on walls; in solitary sarabands
perform till dawn; let them apprehend me
for observation - I'll be dumb you'll see,
when you are one of death's black ordinands.
I shall hurl torches through the burning air;
through a dark forest, like a wounded beast
with nothing now to hold me back, I'll tear;
you will see nothing, once you are deceased;
I'll rage, who cannot find you anywhere,
till I too, blind, deaf, dumb, shall be released.

I stumbled, running, wounded, from those screams,
that spread like fire, behind, ahead, around,
or thrown with fury from deep underground,
flooding the forest with its lava streams,
erasing darkness with its bursting beams,
then slowly cooled till there was no more sound,
and when at last I looked, you were not found,
not in the dark, the daylight or in dreams.
I gave up searching and I saw you fade
to a recumbent shadow with no eyes;
I wondered what it was, this long tirade,
and what the loss, and why the endless cries;
yet as I read it now I'm still dismayed
at your unfaithfulnesses and your lies.

Going mad's not easy - it takes too much time
for those of us who go by rule of thumb
but yet have had enough of being numb
at outrage.
               Your impiety my crime:
I will bury my dead, it is deep in me,
rest I have none, there is no sleep in me
and I have done with dreaming,
I have done with ritualised screaming,
the dead unburied need me for their tomb.

Heed me - I conversation held unsleeping
with ever-unborn whispers teeming in my womb,
that I shall spare from life's uncertain reaping,
therefore all my being their mausoleum.
Creon, for you death waits on policy,
that shall come creeping like your treasurer
with unaccounted woes, your chancellor
with fretting wrinkles from some frontier.

Creon, for me death is the perfect lover,
I know he looks askance upon no other -
Creon, you cannot have my body or my destiny,
though brother to my mother.

Words are most sacred to who know them void:
love is that thing that is no thing except
the thing you gave away because you kept
no part of it that had not been enjoyed.

Can someone make a living out of waste?
Can that be wasted that cannot be made?
Must the dead rise before they can be laid?
Must the sun shine before we can make haste?

These are the thinkings keep me from my sleep
each night as thought of thought of mine will net
each threaded orifice into a threat,
such that, set free, it be not an escape.

Any that named a thing without a name
must take away the missing from what's said
or else mistake the taking for some shame
and saying nothing say that thing instead.

This is the substance hidden from our sight:
only the blind can see without a light;
this is the indescribable unseen,
which words convey, but which they cannot mean.

Should you that must wander alone
by nightfall meet under the tall arms
of a paternal forest a white bird
wounded with thorns,
                    give ease,
take blessing, whereby you will cease
to feel fear at the shade of the trees:

on the eve of your final shrinking
you shall know through the window
the warm wing of that deathless bird
that shall accompany you to the long, grey
vaults of the dead and the never-to-die,
that shall be let loose at last
from the green columns of the cage,
that shall leave indeed empty your round,
bare, dry
            beyond redemption
tampered with head of dissolvable wax.

A form of words only; to give precision
to a passion in the doldrums, hunting a house,
we toed that tight-rope of living-together
through blank streets, taut over map-work
of illumination; a place to set our possessions.
Defeats; growth at a snail's pace. Trail-tread,
this day give us our nightly dead.
Deface. Build a grammatical sentence
to house whose waste? Commonplace,
reiterations, all a matter of, you said it,
taste. Ours is a graphic instinct
to decipher what antrum we think, filtered
through these clauses, beyond causes. Temple-body,
there to worship, let your fingers trace
the conception of an unfamiliar hip.
Sip, gulp, gobble, do not drink. You'll sink.

And this bright consecration
of blessed bread, broken,
to bed: be blissful, it means nothing,
was but a moment out of steam; devotion -
let me show you the level, a bright cluster
of extinguishable moment, followed
by retraction, simple fraction. Add up, multiply,
subtract, divide, right inside. Meant nothing. You do.

This is the echo-chamber, for our bed.
Everybody needs, garden overgrown with weeds,
whatever it was you might have said:
a bright moment, broken, a proffered token,
redeemed, spat wax, thumbed - the past,
preferred spoken, spurred,
                                taken, numbed.

Within the broken heart of ice
is the bruised hawthorn, wherewith
a hermit in this case each day
chewed black roots to cut his tongue
on glass that fell from his eyes -
as you may see depicted in an ornate weaving,
where the glazed lost are irrevocably waving,
where what you may love is cold beyond your touch
under the shrouds of water that wrap you,
such things you may never teach.

That was a root to eat
that fruit sends into the inconcrete mind,
that was to see what see the blind,
what the deaf wait to be told,
that was to hear
as of the lifted up face of the water
that were screwed into a mask of its own deep
regions where salmon are burnished by green
pride of the incorporate sun.

The mind of the black hermit grew scarce
on the burning eyes of the white thorn
so that he must journey through stone
through layers that have crushed forever
the tip of the white wing
till he may find that last sparkling dust
of the ground fossil that shall be let
fly into the scouring wind
and shall fly without falling -
as if the falcon hover for him;
his blood nevertheless shall still grow
on what rock it desiccates
hawthorns out of the iron to sweeten the black air.

I was all day a frozen well,
the unmouthed stones of a roofless wall,
there ran through one the wailing of a bell
away always from the thing it haunted,
against the other that I could not catch fell
the reboundless echo of a lost ball,
that finally I knew I was being hunted -

and looked for you as I have often hinted,
to no avail to know a veil -
I could not pierce the silence of that well,
but dislodged my own voice from dark ledges,
that nested below the level of ice.

Lying on the bed within my cell I heard
a timeless presage of the hurled
shaft of sun:
    are you the white bird of bread
will unhunger us?
      Of your brood
I have stained black the snow
with spilt wine of our healing,
it is I from the chained roots am howling:

oh white bird is it you that have flown
into my eyes as tears,
that have found me
      even in most hidden towers
of the untender bushes,
bird of the incarcerate water I shall not trap
in your head your song that it chokes,
not white perhaps for the tears
have dried on my cheeks
as flowers are touched at evening
by the cold corrector of night.
I must still wait.

Left to peer all day today,
          what else to do,
after the floor of the frozen well
where I am releasing a light bubble of gold;

each time it takes to the air
it sinks under its own weight of black lead,
its yearned-for freedom ore;
I could find no means to rub clear
all that instinct from its dread load.

Being then so many years out of my mind with dolour,
I had acquired a yet unsullied box of water colour
to put the world to rights for a few hours.
To put the world -
                        that is a chaos of uncapturable grief,
how, from the strained windows within which locked,
off the bent eaves I yearned after,
caress essences of form that shall grow softer.

I had been noting carefully all afternoon
those shot-silk pigeons pecking on the roof,
their dislocated rhythms smoothed away
all tugging of reproof that is my bias.
Some can seek solace and high-mindedness
in the tall statues of a virgin marble -
pigeons spatter them,
                        with no respect
for iron heroes never sleeping as they sentinel
our edge of empire city, eyes peeled dry
on introspection, riding their forgotten reputation.

So I was obsessed those hours with pigeons'
restlessness because they talked to me,
because their voices lacked ambivalence,
because I shared the mindless culmination
of their nervings, though they would not pose for me.

Waking, my mind was white, and blank
and full of terrifying hope like this white paper:
then I wished to catch the pigeons at it.
I have passed through every stage of quick
suggestion to release their movement
through my pencil:
                        now I tear the sketch -
they are elusive, they still taunt
my heavy-handed dumbness.

                      I could scream
or I could scatter sentences across a ream
of paper.
               Dark it is -
                      they may have flown away:
but in my mind they left behind
an endless eloquence of droppings,
mostly black, but if I'm lucky,
one smudged memory of graduated grey.

Poetry's too dangerous an instrument
with which to measure our relationship:
if time is tamed by verse into uneasy equilibrium,
what sort of lies would love-lines only foster?

Not to repeat, and not to triumph cheaply,
every poet's chief concern, for which
we would abandon fellowship if that restricts
our mastering conventions. Given so,
a tide that flushed the postures of our limbs last night,
and made a fluid moment of our breath,
would be once only: poets forget
there is a limitation in our possibilities,
of which regret can stifle out affection:

cold ideals from which warm blood retreats,
but eye to eye we see in blindness
if we trust no speech: how from this silence
master selves adrift, unless defeats
are polished on the wheel, and stowed away:
the poet scribbles images that wound and seal.

And any not empirical embrace
could end in strangling, love's white and slender
neck snapped, and the kiss gathered
like a flower, for its smell only and what it says of winter.

Paths split at intervals:
we must diverge according to our calling,
though this wood where we meet
has strange properties of revolving.

tremor left on air after wings scratched sky
night rolling up street like returning sobriety
dawn's dazzling clarities after a sleep
draughted by searching drawers for lost letters
platforms for missed trains
                              crowds for known faces
falling as question mark onto a perch
where the hummingbird stuck
talons of the blood-grave falcon neared
to the singing colours of the small
they swung under trapezing our doubts into a sharp cry
raven opened like an umbrella onto which
hatred poured its object-unspecific powers
exploding as rain that rested the garden
gave it respite to breathe
                              promising a harvest of juices
that even now the stalk took from the soil
to spill into the air without waste
wings winking antenna
                              confirmed things drinking
regardless of how termed
by the precise measurers of data
for whom it is never now but later that we arrive

we slept together fruiting the night
it was the same risk as always
to abandon our separate freight
the ineradicable root
                              my hand in your hair
was a tongue forgoing eloquence

dislodging your eyes like a calyx
I returned to time's temperate dews

My friend and I sat down to drink at table
inside the house; the glass within my reach
I offered shattered. This was the first breach.
We stood outside the house, over the gable
grew a great shadow, falling from a wing
that cut the house in half, voice visible.
I shrank away from it. I was unable.
I heard:
        Give me. I come. I will prolong
no longer. I have come for all first-born.

I rose. I joined a throng of unknown people
that staggered forward.
                And each throat was torn.
We surged together in relentlessness -
what held us back wore faint, was far, felt feeble -
towards the edge of boundless nothingness.

I smelt the grass. It took over my blood,
each vein suffusing with who nourished it
till I was crushed like one stray ammonite
whose bones of weightless understood the blade.
Upwards in-bound, I saw the light un-bend,
talking I heard them what the ancients knew,
all that was left of me flowed into you,
proclaiming only death would seal this bond.

None can assure, the living must retain
separate function of catastrophe
in cycles squeezing foison thorough grain:
priesthood of slaughter fallen onto me;
shall, I enquired, those I know earn peace?
Yes - time perfects.
              But first a sacrifice.

Arches of a deliberate sky, whose corbels we,
may testify to the shade of the cedar
planted on grave cloisters
of procedure, smiles chipped by a chisel
out of the gargoyled rose
at the root of the sacrum.

Channels cannon through winding valleys
of voices whose echoes we catch
as we overlook the edges of immensity.

See, we have sauntered by chance into a tomb
noted for space, never more uncoordinate
than when beneath roofs of an inverted planning:
headpiece our roots.
                        Faces flesh masks not
what made our loathing plot:
whose hearts' refreshing rapids re-sequester
though their blossoms rot,
and leave their memorising under the cheeks,
wrath-tempered stone:
so read my real deceit refracting bone:

out of the howling whence air
withered into gentleness
sprang the begetting;
                        folded to his breast
he overwhelms us, lending us forgetting.

Had you come with me into love's labyrinth
you had regretted its size;
you had found facsimile of death
beneath all pleasure.
You had abandoned all measure
of how far to go
before we know in his not over-reaching intercession

we may miss the meaning of the lesson.

One head that split three ways,
four eyes: two out of every one uncouple.
Upon each sepulchre of fusing hands
I wished your hand in mine
that reaching the vast halls of death
we should walk in, though not in step;

and then I woke with this clear knowledge:
that I was alone, and must walk on,
and you no longer with me;
that I would eventually come through,
you left behind, and only my remorse
to remind of some disturbance, then or now,
something that happened once, I now forget.

My mind breathes ghosts that words cannot unravel,
as I inhabit silence, wearing faith,
so thin a costume I am thought a wraith
but study meanwhile ways of being civil.
Am I responsible for this decline
who am a symptom of my own disease?
Courage I have not - nothing I know frees
what I've become from saying it is mine.

Manners is all, with every word a trap:
obeying gestures borrowed from the well,
I am that tree entranced, but without sap
that points correctly, dead from root to crown,
but I must talk and therefore I must tell
that I am falling upright, standing down.

The truth that you accept shall set you free -
I see it chalked on every racketeer's
bland benefits -
             for you shall lose your fears,
and being no longer blind at last may see
the point of it. What is this hidden knowledge
that has alchemy to change dull substance?
Why have they scalpelled me for innocence,
that see the world as an elector's college
for the endowed?
             Each ex-cathedra pope
has mumbo-jumboed all my murder out -
all their absolving seems to me a grope
after some novelty I cannot share.

I hear their chanting massacre my doubt -
why do they strap me to this writhing chair?

We borrow fingers in default of speech;
pull on gloves to keep our hands from hurt;
we wear each other's bodies and our mouths
may stop us lying if we stitch them so
and stanch what flows in wonder from our lips
to find again we give each other ease.

We wear each other clumsily tonight,
in no performance for applauding cheers,
nor looking over shoulders at ourselves
in postures that might strenuate our loss;
we wear each other heavily, can hardly walk.
The only way to cross the drifting sheets
that we could never read of ice.
                              We try
like children with the finger first across this white.

We have traversed a little of the past,
both blinded by the wastes we cannot speak.
And now at last like penitents are shrift of pose
and lie away unsolid distances;
                          we say it with
our bodies' cruel needs but nothing here is permanent;
if someone saw us now they would believe
the form we take tonight had made us wish
with frenzy we were not mere flesh, mere friable
desire and mere bone, had made us wish
this moment could not break because it took
away the human ache of being alone, had made us
almost confident to speak.
                    But we lie silent. It is better so.

And most of all we fear all promises,
for every promise breaks a net of trust
in which tonight we rest. We hope for sleep,
to wash away these gradual infidelities,

and will not say a word to break the bubble
of illusion on the tongue, for fear
it blister into speech
                    and prove once more
that silent nakedness is out of reach.

No permanent betrothal this, have seen
not caught the flashing wing. Each wonders
what the other really meant
and wishes neither had said anything
but trusted past all reassurances.
                    We hear
the night erode our silences, where darkness
threads the mind. Recumbent body, silence
that I hold within my arms, some ancient code
that must be read by touch, although I am not blind.

the bed I sleep in now
still bears the imprint of your absence
as dew on the grass speaks of sped deer
that at dawn leapt through my garden
their ancient routes
                         beyond a compass logic
air aching yet from their flight

I watched for hours the blue veins
on your wrist slender as petals on which
I rested
         not empty hours I hear
from the lake's closed mind
echoes of angelus running its fingers
through water
                    untidal eloquence
of heart's fibrillation the murmur
I cannot now lodge in your ear
muted as shell might be
in some sequestered rock-pool at evening

NO SUPEREROGATION

Underground streams prefigure a cacophony
when you beat the bounds.
The first deceit is an epiphany
because you listened for sweet sounds.

Your hands grown hot from divination's
twitching fork you follow;
break the rod and in that desecration
you delve beneath to find the rock is hollow.

Then wail and wait for Moses' miracle,
to knock prophetic fists upon the door;
his words complete the ancient ritual
so wail again, and wait, and wail once more.

It runs in trenches to a diamond child
that must be ransomed by a living death,
itself but forfeit for the time when wild
enough to stomach your last breath.

So drink your thirst away. In porcelain?
If you would appetite as shame.
If satisfied, to make you walk again,
unless the mind lays absolute, round claim

to hidden sources, where they gush from fields
in drains that all their bursting saps,
endowing empire on the lord that wields
what golden ramage taps.

The goblet of your blood, drawn from the throat,
must temper restless voices to a sight,
that your being bloodless will in time promote
the things mere bleeding won't requite.

Ah which reclining monarch has not bound
in desecrated courts within chained bowls
he kisses indolently, from underground,
the water's flow: *we learn to bear our souls*,

because his sovereign edict can supply
what it imagines, trusted into touch.
The word being absolute to measure by
is everything that is not much.

Awakened this way by the chanced-on key
what is released must find a human face
to cover it, like bandages, and be
another such, that someone can replace.

Go beat the bounds with honour for the stakes,
and ask who gave us fields and ways to beat:
the stream defines antenna-like that breaks
an open ground, becoming not too sweet.

The one in shackles, now released, pulls through
by putting some identity to shred
new murder:
                  masked, may die, like people do:
for which there must be one unable to be dead.

voices stir this web
a prisoner of eyes I find myself
that look elsewhere
in a perpetual fidget

the hermit shell of words across my back
has grown too tight and squeezes me

I try to fight

too late

I took the bait
of kisses tenderness relief

but unbelief
can only desiccate

KLEIN'S WOES

Sat four hours toying with a negative
to insert for maxim; broke down; lied; wept;
took a wafer of allaying, so slept,
dreamt, woke, wondered, was catechised to live.

Thus the plot for an obituary worked
in the cutting room - sorry, we can't use
it but keep your copyright lest you lose
contact with the mainstream emotion. Jerked

strings through a routine and indifferent
act, backwards projected over groundlings.
Did his turn, bowed, bayed, took a tumble, spent

time post-morteming a deliberate corpse
for glass eye, glazed expression. Other things
such as you might invent for in your cups.

Some sort of periphrasis makes a mark
for the otherwise employed. He indexed
a score of well-intentioned for a text
complexities, such that the undone dark

runs low, unmetered. *Much loved of his friends
to whom...*; in a firm typescript ironed his tongue
out flat, white, seared, what catch, fishing-net lung
on cool-sequestered waterfronts he mends.

Tell us no troubles that we heard before,
the needle's stuck wherewith we sew your eyes
together; if behind the eyes it's sore

with something scratching take a panaceas's

polite injunction borrowed from the wise.
And now they've healed we have to cut your ears.

Living with a perpetual gas-leak
is to wade through hells of tortured desire
and dreaming; freeze on the oiled trapeze wire
from eye to eye, smudge mouths with blood - and speak

heaping the pyramid over a manic
monarch whose laws bind the undeceasing
descendants in a trudge of releasing,
sand through the fingers - tremor beyond panic.

At the appointed hour they all met
for the uprising - to hear the stone drop,
some centuries later send up a wet

confirmation of enlivened sounding;
to which harbingers make a hungry hop,
infer latterly proportioned mounding.

Time is running out for our lovers, boys,
whose hearts grow so large now with love they'll burst
open to show what kept lips so pursed:
no conversation but that bespoken noise

in the night of the warned mouse behind wood.
Who spoke only to the first of the spring's
rash uncouthness for solace: but what things
half-breathed are best glossed over understood -

for sleep may fall overnight like a snow
of untracing, or sleep may burn brightness
out of the grain, or may only ago
brandish and with that wither those blue files

of the ice-mountain in its remoteness,
which is no more nor less to say than smiles.

Drink, was said, this clean water, through the throat
slung knife sharp and blood ran, blood fugitive
as dream to recall when you muscle tough
up to the blue-print morning that plans threat.

That blood was ghost's cloak he wore to wrestle.
Nobody answered the bell, as curtains fell
blood over mind whispering, when will be full
glass head or crack open with tongue's black pestle?

Held sabbath with own invisible priest
spilt from word-roots, derived masters of dumb
fingers sudden on fire; spat the pressed

message out: how weighed in the palm of power;
that wide hall cast vengeance's shadows. Then dim
erasing revealed black caverns of the pure.

In this world a scream transfigured is blood,
as blood in the ear is air being cut red;
that note is a wing that black rays have dried -
soul, if you want it, is what from flesh bled.

Night came on like loss, that is, discover
what you never had: be strong, turn round, face
what you hid from...no tragedy, but farce? -
and knowing what was not could not be over?

Howsomuch each preaches his own bias
of courage, or listens, even the wise
lie as they roll, smile as they pass by us.
The fee for the knife inside, the right voice

is to murder the guilty:

　　　　　　　　your wild woes
are so since others you let wind the vice...

THE LATEST LIE

A parched and speechless mouth, with its tongue tied,
my tremorous body, in that narrow bed,
waiting for you to pour between its lips,
as if to drown the taste of what you said.

That taste makes promises I dare not trust –
I cannot live on tastes, sour or sweet,
I will not ask you what you might have meant,
for anything I asked would make you cheat.

Enduring silence, surely thus no lies
shall flash between us, like the brother's sword?
I slept too long on its bright edge before
and will not sheath it now in any word.

Your room a hollow beggar's countenance,
your bed his bowl – why did I give away
all that I had till there was nothing left,
the room still pleading with me, more to pay.

Had fuller face and more solidity
that room, the silted harbour of my hope;
I waited often for the tide to turn,
to see the busy quayside coiled with rope

that held it to the wharf where it unloads
your promises, those that a child believes,
the happy stories which must wither soon,
the branches bare when they have lost their leaves.

I do not want your promises – just let them go;
they fall like water cupped within my hand,
I bend to drink again, but all is dry,
there are no streams that slide along this sand.

Should I take madness on me like a cloak
and dumbness like a helmet, going blind?
This room is crushing me until I chase
your words and smiles right out of my blank mind.

My fingers scan the lines I have to walk –
must I then cross with naked feet live coals?
The room is rushing with one piercing voice,
its bitter message flickers by in shoals,

the echo ripples through its withering
as clocks cease ticking, running slowly down,
the voice falls silent in this finite space
at last I have become the thing I own.

So read these minutes off; your tongue has told
one final lie as it revolves around
this pale and numbered face you turn to kiss,
you do not notice it has stopped its sound.

I search for you on the blank pages of my days,
but come evening amongst all that scribbling
I cannot find you as you were, no, not a galleon
that wrecked itself on bitter reefs and took its gold
to subterranean shafts of mystery, nor coral even
beneath black shoals of hidden desires, darting like fish.

The mystery is all that's left to me,
and my days move through your obsession
like someone lame learning to walk.
I could compare you for your delicacy to a stalk
of slenderest silver burdened with brown fruit;
for your dark eyes I could command all sorts of birds
to fly, and for your thoughts the moths would serve
that question all perfumes with their daubed wings.

Perhaps for falsehood I should have to think -
so human a betrayal after all that words might fail,
and I might fool myself to say we failed,
and love failed too, and everything had failed.
I wrong you with this rhetoric,
you are more than any image even I could twist
to capture and imprison all sweet agonies.

What can I say, therefore? I put it down like this:
my writing only sweeps away the dirt
from where we have to travel, talking freely,
shall I be happy so to sacrifice the hurt,
and, killing the ideal, to love you really?
Or is this just another exercise
to coin a phrase that covers up your lies?

my pulse you made your own
our bloods beat as one motion
curving through glass
that bends the sun to a golden tongue
destroying what it touches

what need of words -
our bodies sweated tears from wrought flesh
that fell as bleeding in this violence to regain

returning to speech I questioned
was this an illusion

how could we answer
we try to phrase that movement
but how

it has passed out into water
and dissolves

we move on

it was enough
that our pulses once met
in recognition:
                    retained in the visible
they would be lost:
                    renounced
perhaps they keep rhythm

LANDOR ROAD AGAIN

Unclothed killer frisked down with hot hands
more used to counting syllables - that was theory,
this is your beat now, policeman, searching
dishonest flesh for knife or gun,
or in the groin the hand-grenade
that lips must suck, teeth picked by the pin
for all the gold that's there,
                              these buds will burst,
blossoming into stanzas
of a hypothetical yesterday we dare not prove by testing?

We rent our lives on ruined streets,
that bay-window is a mantle of red gauze
over buzzing voices, some party whose vibrations
are the speech of bodies in collusion,
the shared deceptions of sensual betrayal.
And there I imagine your ripe body swinging,
full like a pear that falls from a tree of desire,
into hands that trap, by which you are pared
to a core that is all that is left
upon your departure.
                              Idle reflections,
the sill is a knife, cutting my memories;
I blame the pang of the late lilac,
the dumb snout of the withering senses,
for being unable to uncage from this hollow room
where I float at roof level dreaming of you.

Your excuses now would only substantiate
the betrayal; your assurances
perfect novel gambits towards stalemate.

Our bed a mortice, we in deadlock clinched
the ungiveable

          till we could only take back
things said;
          things done will be swept away
as irrelevant cobwebs by new tenants.

The mattress moulded to our need
and sprang back in the morning.
You live, therefore, your flat day
and lie down in the evening.

Now in this after-midnight aloneness
I tread a causeway towards your beacon,
knowing it was flared by wreckers,
but there are no treasures on my ship,
for I met with pirates.

I passed this coast one night before,
your hands unrigged me with no daintiness.
Shall I return?
          Shall I leap falls for you,
is it the right river, known for certain
by the way I edge into it,
without having to find my direction,

and what if you are not there,
and for how long am I making this up,
and if I turn from the window what shall I see?

winking was sunlight in the high window
as I stroked your head those nights
wrapped in your limbs
                              in wild sea-weed tangled
the ways of your unspoken darkness

there were dawns hatching from egg-shell
to the blue rhythm of your breathing
my eyes blinked from broken pieces of sky
falling over the tree-tops
what sun uncoiled wings from the fragments
with pale feathers
                              nestling to be fed my hopes
that I had found from you

not now but from all corners the dry cough
of cars
            a different breathing of traffic
scratching the roads
the room chambers their echoes
bright-head no more on my shoulder
browsing your aching meadows of sleep

I held you only as clearings contain sunlight
and coming through columns of darkness
I found you had flown
and the sound of my own unmeaning

I have not talked away the stone
you fed me as I beseeched you with slight fingers
running through stalks of your hair

The things not said
speak most
                not loud but with authority

I read between the lines of your unsent letters
I scan between the lines of your unsaid regrets
I search between the broken promises
I look into the darkness behind eyes
I fathom the silence within ears

I am left holding together an empty room
with my bare hands
                        whose walls and roof are my head
whose floor has fallen and I with it

but I must not let this room collapse
lest it raise dust and splinters
that could irritate your passing eye
or sting beneath your nails
if you were walking by

THE SHRINES OF FREEDOM

A week ago I remember the cow-parsley choked
on its own sensuality, the nettles
promised ungiven kisses a week hence.
Always circling, the midget planes
dropped invisible bombs we were trying to forget.
Bombarded nevertheless with indubitable calamity,
we held hands. You said: *it's almost idyllic* -
meaning that in such a paradise
the separateness of lovers could still sting.
I drank from a trough with old water in it.

Picking up flints chipped into axes
you reminded me of their users:
we smiled at the flints we kept behind our eyes.
They were here then, you said, *now we pass.*
Suddenly we clutched at each other.
Then evening began to unwind
its skeins into the orchard.

One day, perhaps, these words, fractured
into crude sense of cutting, may fall
into excursioning hands, though not yours,
to occasion some remark, as

they must have served some purpose long ago,
museum pieces now of an old culture,
and did they think as we do,
with such under-developed instruments
for the perfection of pleasure?

I wait for your voice on the phone,
the familiar dread at those clipped syllables,
the cadence as cool as a snake in water,
the rich coils of your twisting my gullibility
pulsing faintly, that is, your pauses
into which I rush as soldiers into a breach
to be blown up by bombs.

Your voice on the phone is thunder and lightning,
the gap between them widens each time.
Your voice that I wait for is a vulture,
my sense of it curled in the dormant phone
like a seed grown in a jar,
                    what green tooth will jut
from the gums that bleed and cut
and fang into water - what sweet fronds
deceive but for the glass,
what poisoned flower chewed by silence
to spit in my eye?
                    How could the harsh sound
be sweet that brings me your voice,
you will purr into my ear but I know the claws.

But surely vultures circle till the beast is dead?
You won't ring yet. But I know you well enough,
and even now your finger
moves like a shadow round the dial
and I feel myself shrink to a dry carcass.

DOUBLE DUTCH

Courage, paying, any double-dealing language
that sounds better the less it means
is to the English Dutch and to the Dutch English.

My Dutch wife to the Dutch would be English.

We accept the substantive but quarrel
over quality embodied in the epithet - take courage,
or cowardice: English cowardice
to the English is Dutch, courage, that is,
when it does not need to be named except
by the Unenglish when it is not of course
courage but presumably to the Dutch
courage if the English are right.

Dutch uncle, perfect in balance,
paying the invoice without looking,
waving flunkeys away with a tip.

Dutch wife, beautiful eyes; busy, confusing
hands, a thousand lies behind the face
that closes up like a flower when night comes.

Not to be trusted, especially when smiling.
To sleep with it and stroke its hair,
silver and black, as midnight drunk with cold stars,
Dutch wife, loving with Dutch courage,
lies in Dutch, you must speak Double-Dutch
if you would understand why the Dutch wife
remains so silent, does not seem to know who I am,
pillow or bolster, each gratefully sinks into
a sort of comforting collusion.

These stranded lights across the valley
tendons are of an unpunctual ghost
that must be stretched
as cats and souls are said to be
(and one of these to body out of all eternity).

A cramped proportion! Yes. My diaphragm
could be your sort of cradle.
Preaching caution, as for an investiture,
I time this solid monarchy with pulses;
could conclude: as last, not as before,
you have turned up again
with all that panoply of stating choices -
battleships and cruisers striking out
the strategies of pain. That will not be.

This, then, by which the voice divorces
sense from sounds as I require
unrebuttal,
                your perpetual disdain;
you mark the out of bounds I'm almost into.
What is to make of all these ironies
and this their preface not unwittingly?
What sort of unrequital?

Why should we bother with an under-dress-rehearsal?
Simply, softly tell me what I have to hide.
To end on some remark: all this is only chance.
I would have said some people kiss
to bite. You said it first:
that some must scratch to write.

there is no future but a past unravelled
I am the cage of the maimed beast
trying to remember its boast
till all lies revealed

there is no past but a present that's void
of all structure
                    thus we catch hold
of a wound that we think has healed
and find it still open whereverfrom viewed

there is no present but the shadow of pain
as though that proved body and light
somehow I find I am still afloat
I confirm myself with the tip of my pen

there is no me but a pen in my hand
all is brute
                    with every reprieve
I run as somehow I could reprove
a self by a pursuing hound

KLEIN'S DREAM

have shed their wings as clothes the black dreamers
bind back eyes
                    your immemorial feet
of Chinaman in a clock

going round the hours to look for a baby lost
that time has mechanised

the hare you chase is one black pupil
this is certain
                  playing marbles with their eyes
behind the curtain what do they choose
if not the treasured prize

white blood thaws in my mind with shock
I move down the lanes
as indiscreetly as voices on wires

I struggle with my hopes like a wrestler
dripping oil
              can find no hold
but slip about my thoughts
and like a ship gored by a horn of dearth

white horn gashing the water
spun from the lurking killer

behind my throat

there is no silence
but one by one they struggle back
the broken soldiers of words repulsed

how shall I feed that horde
of my conquered troops
whilst the victorious adversary
lays siege to my waking

there is no one to surrender to
but the white wind that needs me to eat
to preserve
                its lack of all substance

beat my brains with your eyes
devour myself
                I hear your speech
as the echo of splinters that bombed my flesh
I was not there
                your presence the hearse
of my pain
                I give wreaths of smiles to the priest

you accompanied my absence
as far as the gate and left
now each step is the mirror that trapped
like a web myself
                and I cannot move
from the image but let time stretch

all traverses I make for melt
the mind-broken rope-bridge made of words
you cannot cross now nor jump
but walk down gently into the empty
hole of your self and wait
                for what?
some companion to help pick from your dead flesh
the bruises of smashed words

on which you walked through air and fell
removing even
                    the blank space of the grave
that gives you shape
who cannot howl but mouth
                    being dead

words are flesh that clothe no spirit
to cross war-theatres takes steps forward
into the grave
                    there are orders
to move consolidate retreat
post-mortems make a triumph or defeat

in my head the bayonet the organ of balance
I have slit often the throat
                    of my own shadow
felt thereby ensuing blood of air
that dries into shock to make sense
of discarded selfhood with flesh with words
eyes are mirrors that do not release
what passed before them locked in a trap

Neither was truthful or honest:
the other was not enough,
but we could not let go.

A constant struggle,
this dissatisfaction,
against being alone.
                              So we put up with it
and called it love;

defeated in the end,
by all that hedgehog-spine, gooseflesh
excitement at the unknown,
those ragged, rough desires
one could not own,
till it was too late to forgive,
to accept, to belong –

a fallen moment, some defiant song
tells me to bear it out
and find a way to stroke still your hair;

but you are now a figment,
trapped in my lines,
and I am mouthing syllables to someone
far removed from all this rigmarole,
who cannot hear,

so, despite poetry,
there is no way to connect,
now as it was then.

CONVERSATION PIECES

What is it between you - are you lovers?
And what are lovers, I reply:

we have too much detachment, we pass
as ships in the night, all lights blazing,
the horns goading us forward into the dark
till left with only our own echo and the sense
of a ghost that motions the water,
memories of a familiar substance,
anecdotes of the lack of touch.

We succumb to our charms, keep out of sight
the snake, we believe our stories,
unverifiable as an old photograph, certificates
or worn clothes gathering dust, our disarticulating
bones fleshed by our warmth, each soul
a figment of the other's mind.
Understanding, and kind, gentle, with no demands,
we are sorting it out, swapping anxieties
like stamps of a new country.

A new country! Yet so quickly passed through!
Not to explore beck-gullies matted with years of leaves;
cliffs of cloud above clouds of cliff; graveyards
in the stern garden whose stone faces
propped on old pillows stared away
from the winding road to the windows
where others missed them and peeped
incredulously at old tombs.
                              My body is failing,
I thought, *sooner than I imagined*, but wrily added,
my body has always failed me,
this just another trick of the light of time
to warn that it's getting darker,

everything runs out of time in time.

One day shall meet on soft foothills,
pure in our general love, debate
essential fractions of the way, mouthpieces
of the spirit, shall talk,
our words circling the hills - windows
onto the infinite, stars nailed
into doors that will not open.

Anything we might say would falsify,
we are too adept at metaphors, speak too well
this soft communing, matching with insight,
eloquent, oblique and smile a lot -
and into our dreams will unreel
that new-found place, a landscape
without symbols -
                    stripped of all intent to deceive,
words falling like snow to dampen the echo
of hard-won breath, till now, advantage-point,
all lays itself bare beneath us:
a valley and its river, the tumbling mist;

and each turns to go, wondering how to greet
when we meet again, no longer flesh and bone,
freed of the taut paleness that stretches
the base of your skull, that tendon
rivering under your hair, awaiting an axe,

the gesture I did not make despite my tenderness,
to stroke your neck where your head
                            is bridged to your spine.

So, I must pick my way through Latin verse,
following phrases as they buck and bend
in rhythms that distemper or distend

to resurrect a multitude from terse

directions in the drama we rehearse;
to guess at more than I can apprehend,
whose only meaning is the way lines end,
with crippled rhymes that mirror my remorse.

Gnawing dead bones with nothing left to eat,
old echoes of a music I have lost,
frustration's flesh, the repetitious beat

with which the silent spaces are engrossed
till sound like sense itself grows obsolete -
what else is this, but choking on a ghost.

We should meet by chance,
some years after we kissed,
and in the clamour of that bar
I would stare at you,
                          loss grabbing my throat
like, they say, a cornered rat -

something prevents returning,
those shared secrets
whispered these bodies as water falling,

something denies the pure laughter
of then being one,

now strangers greeting

though were I alone
I would grab you as my only companion,
in shock, and shaking my head,
disbelief in these customs and time,

excitedly crying:

that was no dream but real
you did not hear
and now strangers only
we are skirting the night.

It should be possible to remind -
how you fingered my pliant moan,
finding a diverse speech others could ponder:
we spoke only in open adoring
of these drab lines,
                    our-to-be-given-bodies,
despite all differences, a wonder,
an immensity and yet a narrowing
as though smiling were part of our limbs,

and the eyes drank me into knowing
that death's caress, gentle as this,
were now proving my petty needs
ample as leaf, your cheeks my breath

and both blown by a touch -

falling my windfall fingers
into a bruised loneliness, seeming not yet alone,

all senses down, memory of sensation,

to questions, on waking, what is life anyway

or

after-such-wandering-without-you-what-am-I?
tongues for speaking dumbly
for mute choruses

                    moved to that chasm
the abrupt declivities ferny and bright

where water-laughing lightness left out
the deep-mining-and-brilliant-in-darkness-core
that laps richness from these workings

tongue of our language
brutal and at the root straightforward

what layers of meaning
I could lick where your moaning illumination

extinguishes as it lights up
my darkest
                    and most unspoken thought

into endless orifice

Then who am I talking to?
Is it really you, some survivor
of those times we barely needed talk
because touch spoke,
our voices confirming what else sang.

Times change:
                    the withdrawing tide
gradually shrank away,
you became pale, and petulant
my requirements of you -

as there are pools left
where trapped fish flounder,
bewildered and exhausted,

a last-gasp-love.

Ignore at your peril ghosts, such as seen
in smiling photographs, and wonder
why it was false, the smile, or what lay
behind the facade of trouble, weathered well,
for that person is long dead, the image
in black and white a fossil only -
                                though they tease
the imagination, these carbon resurrections
of what had meaning only because
it was transient;
                    passing has virtue -
these immortal mouths and their prison-eyes
trap memories; walk past, avoiding the gaze.

The house has ached with moments
gathered at random;
                        a look or a chance phrase
that echoed in endless ricochet,
waves moulding the shore, each ripple of tide
is a fossil of some falling sigh:

let me transfer your smile
soluble as clouds in a dark,
a murderous sky.

Sorry to leave you, but sorrier still
I cannot leave behind these ghosts you will become,
each time I pass cut grass they will rise like damp,
the ache that each year deepens
bleeding into itself.
                        I want no photographs,
of these days, these nights we spent together,
such are pale when compared with the printing
of touch on my nerves;

                              blame, if you must,
the drowning in drink, the loss into work,

but let me tell you this:
                              it was not I
abandoned what I love; I took my time
and stood and nursed my hurts
and waited for remorse to bring them back.

But no-one came;
                              and after waiting in the dark
morning convinced me it was no mistake,
for they had gone.
                              I shall survive again,

and does it matter, anyway,
for I am safe in a familiar pain.

DREAM HOUSE

Deserted when we passed,
the house is mine -

only the ghosts
of those who loved there

tired eyes strained seawards.

At the window
I hear waters where I played

deceived again by pain,
believing I am not alone.

Mine,
the haunt, hiding from the sun.

These crooning cadences do not caress,
are just a background as I sit alone,
they make an echo while I pick a bone
with my dry lover's ghost I can't undress.

Why did you die, but do not fade away;
what did I fail to do or did amiss,
what is the reason I have come to this,
torn from my dreams to the cold light of day?

I've made an empty cavern of my mind,
and found it flooded, till it flickers out,
the candle in the cave I left behind;

the shadows stumble blindly through my head
till they dissolve in questioning - I doubt
if I can warm the ghost I take to bed.

I did not see the bird that sang
the song that gave me pause:
  without a word
             I felt and heard
its cold remorse

I took that message to my heart
and tried to understand
  what I would give
             the one I love
who held my hand

as though my hand would keep you safe
then when you grasped it tight
  and other such
             your hand would clutch
to your delight

But you let go and so you fell
and lost all innocence
  cast adrift
          to slip and shift
through your lost sense

Is there a moral lovers all
who see the lover perish
  when it's done
            sigh for the fun
but do not cherish

here at last words are superfluous
sense left to the eyes
touch wondering finds stone warm
angles of sunrise contrived compasses
as shadows point a pivot
in the giddy clock
that marks off losses
                              marks of losses
night after night memory-less
eaten have slow their worm-kiss
out of rock local
the speechless act of two and two
is one is only ever one is everyone
aware is one invisible
and desperate disparity
which brings us back alas
                              alas
to what exactly did you mean by that
obsessed you did not think it so
crossed swords cross words
                              crosswords
except he cannot spell
who cheats at clues to spoil
compiler and creator god
who only edits us
when we are dead
pretending then
to know no punctuation
stepping-stones of sense

stone stops

BEFORE THE MIRROR

actors mimic their own distress,
stored for a time
to be unfolded before audiences
eager as lovers to be surprised
by the fruits of frequent rehearsal;

poets unclothe themselves in caves,
damp and uninhabitable,
hoping to fill the blankness with echoes,
trapped orgasms, their wasted lives,
moving on from the empty cobwebs at last
they pass round amber verses,
lay down the beds of their archives,
the dull thump of verbs
pounding our temples:

Had there been an outlet
for this grief into your body,
they strum, *I should not*
have needed the elaborate
artifices of likeness,
                              to strike these attitudes,
actor over the blank whiteness,
distributing passion in leaflets,
or at readings, to those avid for meaning,
tinkering in public with my own bad
plumbing, the rushing cistern
trickles through my hot-tap-voice,
with its worn washer.
                              High-class whoring,
and why not, we all sell what we have,
hands and feet, it's an open market,
prizes going to the best bidder.

Phone calls that never came,
footsteps that proved
to be only dead leaves
scraped by the wind,
dead lives,
waiting for someone, always,
with the imagination
to suffer our indigence.

No! I pay out means
to keep you smiling, thus,
my tranquil lovers,
fat in your cells,
sleeping off the hunger
till you are full-winged
and fly to mate.

Good Dr Brown,
cross as a lord,
with seemly frown
saw to his ward-
   the king of hearts;
there, as he trod,
a patient farts,
who can't afford
consultant arts;
non-paying sod
   affronts the god.

Thus each departs
in fits and starts,
   to private pain -
will god-Brown gain
his just reward?
From spluttered plea?

How long, oh Lord?
Before my fee?
I have to keep my family.
Whose fault was that,
   spat neutered cat.

The doctor has a new cravat.
We all must die. It comes to that.
Pray when at last you must go down
   it be not under Dr Brown.

Two caterpillars, eggs adjacent laid,
met on the leaf through which they crawled to light,
and were companions in appetite,
just munching leaves till they could be re-made.

Would-be neotenous, with aching need
towards the other, they must fornicate;
but insufficient means to replicate
meant sighs: they sought in vain to set their seed.

No way to couple!
                  We shall find a way
when we have mating organs, butterflies
whose wings are strengthened by the growing day.

And so they search and do not recognise
each other in the fluttering of May
when every flying creature multiplies.

Suffer, bright silence, my shrill scrutiny;
that trembling tenement, was it you turned
in your indignant grave?

                    Ignominy
has pushed your lady from the stage. They learned
from your fanatic heart but mutiny
and uncompassion. Therefore, when they burned,
the heart they sacrificed, the stream-borne stone
was smashed to bits, its splinters human bone.

Ireland won't hear you - in their ears the roar
of secrets stutters from no sea-worn shell
you saved and polished from a crumbling shore
to teach respect. Old spaeman, cast your spell
like bread on water for the waves to gnaw;
it is too late to argue with Parnell -
does he rub shoulders now with Gladstone there,
and do they vie, as who should take the chair?

England, the honest broker, makes an end
of stringing continental kings; she deals
with Europe as an economic friend,
exchange of honour and of automobiles
must prove that time and indigence will mend
quarrels and interference;

                         at her heels
Ireland still snaps, whom England loves no less:
she'll find some sop to offer Cerberus.

That Tone bequeathed his self-inflicted wounds
to all that follow, passionate, public men,
exultant tongues that detonate the tunes
of glory.

              They'll storm heaven; in their train
the maimed will stumble through the waking ruins
to put to sleep the people in their pain.

And god, who did it once, in Jericho,
does it again, this time in stereo.

Milton, if he were living at this hour,
could trace how Satan flourished in his fall,
and tutor Cromwell, for the ivory tower
has crumbled to a single wailing wall,
that echoes back the straining breath of power.
Better it seems, then, not to talk at all -
I am naive, old master, in such things
whose eyes are clouded by imaginings.

You saw it and your vision had some vogue
with tutors dusting their integrity;
the manger-changeling proved a wounded rogue
that trampled underfoot each century.
You added your excesses to the brogue
of cluttered catches we call poetry,
and dug the middle ground, to cultivate
the roots of passion, lest they grow to hate.

Though it be still to haver at despair,
though no one listen, deafened by the screech
of human-mocking voices through the air,
though we are numbed, we must grope back to speech
between each other, some demolished prayer
of naked meaning -
                    shall the poet preach?
And if he stutter they will laugh to scorn
unnatural birds that fly upon the thorn.

Some write to verify, or vindicate,
describe, denounce, and others of us try
to beat the time before it is too late,
which is unjointed, tapping on the thigh
iambic geldings, wading through a spate
of muddied waters hoping to defy

the tide. Dull blankness speaks the most distress,
this chatter measures out our unsuccess.

Well, are you restless, have you plugged your ears
against the sirens' strain that never fades?
To hear their voices moves the strong to tears,
or, if you live today, introits police raids.
The hag is loose on us,
                              electioneers
for freedom; who give way to her she beds
and mirrors them their faces, petrified,

and having done,
                         she tosses them aside.

Thrashing, fish in my net,
you are caught in my arms
and then you are mine,
bright track of moonlight,
searing the water,
                    what,
shall I pull through your lips
the hook of my kiss,
leaving you stunned by the light
of the sun
            to gasp your last
breathless spasm of flickering scales;

you squirm as my hands embrace -

had you bitten, I mean.

The smell of soap lingered
all day, troubling as a dream
half-remembered.
                              Traps
set by a quizz-wizard,
these memorial hauntings,
along dark corridors,
it reminds of something:

suddenly shafting as bright sunlight,
the broken dream, the recollection,
that was not my body, mist over a river,
hiding the water, that insistent reminder -

the soap
with which I had washed
when I woke;
                          the smell
of a body not my own,
intangible as music,

though I had often touched it,
and knew full well the means
to make it play.

A SOLITARY ORGASM

Late summer, sea-side, when the lights
came on - the promenade had ribs
that spluttered fire - the sudden shock,
when not expecting it,
                              gratuitous
illumination, a spendthrift symbol,
had we seen it then, throwing light
on our relationship, and how
we switched each other on,
to feel the needle scratch out
floating melodies and see you see
my face distort
                    at my own body's need
to need your own.

Winter, the promenade now abstract;
 I tank myself with beer
                              too drunk
to wank, I fall asleep in self-caressing arms,
moulding you out of empty air,
theoretical and comforting,
round which the mind can curl
like tongues of sea
                    under the cold breakers
with their foaming teeth
that gnaws beneath the pier
where I sit without you
gulping beer;
                    and I relapse again
to poetry as a penance for the way
that certain shapes beguile me.

I always hoped the verse
might mute the thirst, make it acceptable,

or else before the mirror I rehearse
the proud performance of my slight relief
and practise ways to make you tremble,
lonely, repetitious, brief -

now with my fingers I remember you
and for a time transform
                              the moment
if I am not drunk enough;
                              risking the distaste
of those I write for

suffering themselves this sense of waste.

JARDINE MATHESON

It's up for grabs, the Brits are moving out,
let Hong Kong settle on its base of greed;
the Chinese want it back and will, no doubt,
manage to manage it within their creed.

In the great boardrooms tai pans flick their ash,
gently caressing tongues lick velvet gold -
Hong Kong is ours, let go, we want the cash,
in this transaction every soul is sold.

Polite decorum decorates the thrust,
naked, as ever, at this surest deal:
leave it to England to abuse the trust
again, that when it cannot buy, will steal

away, that is, its tail between its legs,
but walks, as always, with its head held high;
and what it left behind was just the dregs:
ourselves an island, it was worth a try.

But other islands are not sold so cheap,
we go to war sometimes, sometimes back down;
no matter that the look-outs fell asleep -
the lion has roared, the Brits have come to town.

Rejoice, rejoice, we have reclaimed that land,
exultant triumph, we have righted wrong,
and let dictators tremble at our stand,
as we stood by the people of Hong Kong.

Jardines, who live to fight another day,
will move if must its office somewhere new.
England will bleat about the English way
with great conviction: let the Chinese stew

in their own juices: let them save their face.
We'll put our ships to sea, prepare to fight
to save a handful of this scattered race,
heroic Britons to the last, and white.

THE CONCERT OF EUROPE

Wiener Kongress, piecemeal la paix de Versailles,
the Concert of Europe, in full orchestra -

who is conducting, Napoleon or Hitler,
and other less ambitious would-be madmen,
(though not Stalin), who tore up maps and histories
as they trod down former frontiers of prejudice:

by now Alsace or Elsaß, Lorraine or Lothringen, -
who cares - Riquewihr or Reichenweier,
backwards and forwards, the nesting stalks,
à peine placed, kaum mindful of accents,
emblems all the same of a pride in small places,
in languages only their own,
and a hatred of strangers,

which some Europeans do not feel
at this time when borders dissolve
without enmity, in an idea
of working and living together,
bound up with Schiller and Goethe,
                              good Germans;

staring out of us into great possibilities
of wholeness, wondering whose the armies that over-ran
and what possessed them in their impossible rampage;
and for all that foresight unable to see the future
where devils pranced, as they did in his work,
though different:
                    could he imagine those dark days
ahead, where his own words were twisted
without compunction into a strident creed?

Your pain hurts more than my own
because I can bear my own pain,
since I do not have to imagine
but endure:
　　　　　　your pains are not
an endurable experience for me,
and I have to imagine them,
but also powerless,
by my endurance of pain
to pass on to you
　　　　　　　　the blank acceptance
of my unimagined pain.

I offer practical solutions
and anodyne,
　　　　　　for it is no good saying
I could die for you, as once again,

I would endure nothing,
released at last from imaginary pain.

DOG BITE

You raised your hand to my neck,
and nipped me there, to illustrate how dogs
bite at that point and fling rats in the air.

I've seen the dog race down the yard,
snatch at the scurried, fleeing, futile rat,
running with all its speed, the dog cumbersome
with clumsy, comfortable weight, but accelerates,
lopingly, and catches, captures, then lets go,
tossing this verminous-plague-purveyor
with a footballer's feint over its head,
up-and-over, Garryowen-rat,
Black Death and pestilence up in a blanket -

was there time for a complaint-cry,
some squeak of recognition, or did I imagine
the squeal, the simple reaction
to a nerve cut dead,
an articulation that ran out of time.

And you, with your hand on my neck,
still squeezing, to show how it's done,
stroking, as it turns out,
                          never that dispassionate
precision of the right place to formalise rodents,

disposable flesh, smiling as you caress,
and the dog shows no further interest in the chase
and is bored with athletic hindsights,
and no desire to eat what made
those limbs leap into action.

Bad film, bad processing,
but not the light itself:

a tippex blob eradicating time,
erasing loss across the sound.

Memories presented from negatives;
someone will someday
                              cast
these photographs aside.

Faces and landscapes;
alter and stay the same
                              at a different
pace of time.
                    But have you not,
in glancing at a child,
seen in her fold of eye, her fall
of cheek, a ghost
in fading photographs,
or in that ghost's diaphanous, dead eyes

seen the reflection
of a smiling child?

ROBIN'S PINCUSHION

Robin who? Redbreast? Rouge - heraldic
or cosmetic, thorn-blood, prick
your sensitive finger; or Goodfellow, Puck,
mischief-monger, cell-chaos; calm this speech,
don't over-react, tumorous individuation
rocks us all, we must collect ourselves,
petals are dry-brown, hip-heavy,
stem-leaves, though blotched,
still vigorous.
       *Chemically induced
distortion of leaf buds,* I read, *caused
by the parthenogenetic hymenopteran
gall wasp* - four transparent wings,
I know that thing, have been its host, but here,
a profusion of wild growth, at first blush beautiful,
flower or fruit, yet neither. How does a dog-rose
deal with the delicate, dirty sting of warm eggs;
but to go berserk, crabs itch on the stalk, mutate,
transform, - if god has eyes they tremble
at light in mitochondria, peer way beyond now,
not what is seen, but sight.

How does the rose, love's thug,
hybrid and pampered, bred to a perfect pitch,
devoid of vice, survive such a crude assault?
I'm for the wasp but not against the rose.
I do not understand how grubs
will come to breed again, or how the rose
turns leaves into a fibrous whirl of red,
and this blind wriggling
will, or would, if I'd not brought
their slight throbbing into my reason's knife,

fuse with another stem in sickness and in health.

THE ANGEL OF DEATH

wing-tips envenomed,
dips and soars, wears cloaks, surprises
as she, it, he, masturbates our losses
into portents, forebodings, fates -

how false, though, astrology, if mating
predicts,
                    planet eggs bombarded
with inevitable debris
from exploding accumulations of dust.

Not always stranger, or danger, swift,
curves this brief visiting to mark doors
or foreheads, but, daily bread as familiar,
settled at your table, in your bed,
inexorable as comfortable, slow buttering,
echoing snores, companion, smell-safe,
reliable, familiar, relievingly contrite,

usual conclusions of the same dispute -

the angel is disguised in this daily hunger-itch
of the wasp-instituted eating away of us,
till we are emptied of even regret,
which we took for the gnawing,
not even a vacuum left by the rushing of wings,
faint-etched possibilities unhappened,
unfelt absence, remorseful, but sexless, stealth,

for parasite love only, of course, I speak,
not knowing other, but I have read of it,
and in my neighbourhood we get by
on feeding ourselves at best,
not boasting and safe in our beds,

having long woken to know that we sleep
with the Angel of Death,
                              a drugged,
late-summer wasp which cannot harm -

how can I love except the struggle
we seem to share, to care
for the exhausted pest, the mirror I beseech
showing me only
                    the Angel of Death,

who did not seem to eat me then,
at that old encounter
                    but waiting for now.

Pubs, as you well know, if you frequent them,
are like Parliaments, places
of great pronouncement;
                                    laws
are laid down; truths, which may well
be no more than abominable prejudice,
are explosively propounded; and a careful,
judicious and sensitive analysis
of the conditions under which we all live,
is carried through under the bellicose,
because wronged, hospitality of a landlord
whom Chaucer knew, and Shakespeare
and Dickens, as he weaves his listeners
into a net or web of his own resentments -

voting for authoritarian principles,
but himself a victim, and by the very
partiality of his audience giving the lie
to that strange, mad woman who wandered in
one evening off the streets and screeched
with such volubility that there was
no such thing as society.
                                    At which
she was promptly excluded from this
close company of complainers
and cast out into the streets she once owned
but declined to maintain
                                    bawling with hot cats
the unsolid lava of her certainties.

Take a sponge or a brush, squirting some foam
on the spot, and rub and wrist -
it will come out.
                        Death does that -
you search for the stain on the carpet,
but there's no fingerable blemish now,
the bulb has gone,
disconnected telephones have their own sound.

I saw him put in the ground,
but months later I tried the number,
just in case they'd made a mistake.

But it was all efficient,
a clear message in my ear,
one of those noises that means,
if you look it up,
                        in their book,
that nobody's there to answer,
the digits removed from the market.

I read stains with reverence,
I know just what the mark on the carpet
meant at its time
                        though now it is part
of the texture of things,
part of the dirt, part of the general grime.

GOOD HOUSEKEEPING

On some September day
the mice come inside:
it tells us that summer has finally gone by,
though it does not yet portend the cold
and the dark - they know what we forget,
not calendars, but instinct in the air,

                       and everywhere

they leave the trace
of their insistent presence:

scurry and stealth, bright morse
of the changed weather, this sharing
of house-need, as Burns knew, no matter
how many we have trapped
with a steel jaw snapped
over their neck or back,
breaking this restless, breathless
running of time,

          and still, each autumn,
to our food-rich, enormous, vengeful
executions, our species-specific encounters,
they come in

        and seem for a while at home,
but there is no social union, no symbiosis, nor even
live and let live:

        lightly annihilated by pest control
as part of good housekeeping.

             One time,
the trap didn't kill outright, - crippled,
rear legs limp, it had manoeuvred
over the edge and paddled in circles
across the floor:

         I wondered:
how does one deal with this?

Your words still sting,
though photographs, if I had such a thing,
would be faded now and folded away,

they would not say
how you felt, but how I see
a caught moment, a rare smile, or a pose -

these things are not,
                    for you rot
in ground made somewhat monumental,
with your name, but no dates

and I still cling,
though I know you are dead,
to a stroke, almost asleep,
                    of a head,
mine it could be, or yours,
or anyone else, for that,

so long ago now, nothing belongs,

whatever, whenever we played on that bed.

Siblings womb-share diffidently.

Do we ever remember?

Shell-tenants, temporary, borrow home -
who crabs surer in ever-expanding,
ever-dividing solitude,
                              the vomit of god,
with its mean and solitary eye
watching the dice fall
from his single claw,
                    her folding-in,

not one, but several, they wish,
bored to tears by their blood in game,
appeased
            when there is no control
and they enjoy disappointment,

not the cold monuments of their indifference.

The beat will fathom or the beat will drown:
death as the officer will take aside
my memory, my flesh, will take me down,
and you, not I, will know that I have died.

Some quiver in the leaf or stream, some tide
that trembles, echoing some fuller moan,
as fecund fuels itself to suicide,
some water troubled still by far-flung stone,

reborn to do again all that it did,
which means I shall not have you as my own,
never to join. I am dispirited,
taking our ways in parallel, alone.

How shall I know, if it is all so sweet,
whose blood between whose legs gives out this beat?

THERAPIST

Hague of our salvation,
does not condemn
immoral or unnatural sex as wrong,
but as unhealthy.

A man of substance,
not fat I would call him,
but well-proportioned,

kind he says my words are
and I continue uncomfortable
in sharing a different perspective,

my instincts troops under his direction,
courage and judgment,
poppy, cock, and balls
all jumbled up:

le diable n'est pas mort, it seems,
because *il n'y en a pas* –

that is, there isn't one;

it's up to me to shake him off
and thank the lord and master of our lives
that he is gone.

JUST AN OLD TOOL BOX

A decent time we waited to dispose,
given away or sold, all his belongings,
what he'd owned, to close
accounts and clear the head.
This guarding of un-needed things
slow sapped a second time to make him dead.

Rusty and stained, *this bag of tricks* remains,
which almost any twisted key unlocks,
in spreading drawers retains
a tool-made world that tells
inside this battered magic box
of dormant, hidden, once exploding spells.

Some pairs of pliers; in their canvas pack
two sets of screwdrivers; set-square and rule;
we kept the workbox back;
his hands, it seems, still hold
each rusty, cherished tool
with which the meaning of his life is told.

I might make sixty: twice as old as you
with your two hundred years and more to watch
post-mortem pleasuring. I feel your touch
always; and antenatal; we were two

who throbbed together and each other knew,
though single then, and now; how can we match
unsubstanced souls, unless the skin to scratch;
echoes unsmell earless that eyes unview.

Not what we see at all, but how, the wise
say in unworldly warning to the weak;
the world a curtain woven out of lies,

but lifted up by vacuous technique;
how do we see each other without eyes
and without mouth or tongue how do we speak?

Tchaikovsky, turbulent, plaintive,
desperate,
        hackneyed in falling pitch,
keighleyed in cloying sentiment, akin
to a pain-bellow of solar-plexus betrayal
into nothing;
        the dark gasp, the gap unbridgeable,
abîme, Abgrund, пропасть, αβυσσος, תהום, -

that would do - to drop down to extinction
and lights out, dark tingling
with seaweed-memories, pool-filling
moments of magic and prestidigitation -

we can make you all disappear -
fainter, yes, but not verschwunden
as words swim out of their territorial
vocabulary and we all drown
in a welter of
        what-did-he-say-
to-hurt-what-was-it said-to-me-that-time
-that-still-stings-and-

wallowing, the weight is too much
and we sink down, down,
with nothing worked out,
                replete, historical,
unnerved, on an ocean bed settled,
slow oxidising, we rust up,
                disintegrating,
rotting away, skeletal, finally forgetful,
dementia a state of grace.

The alien looked disconcerted when I said to -
but there isn't an appropriate pronoun
in our language yet - when I said
that a major theme of literary discourse
in humans was the battle of the sexes.

'Fighting is gender-based?' The alien
had been learning English from selected texts.

'Sometimes it is, I think...but the clash
or conflict between men and women, resolved or unresolved,
is said to be at the heart of...well, everything, probably.'

'Gender for you is a category in the modes
of reproduction;
                  it seems to cause trouble;
for us it is a stage in the search
for enlightenment, that can be attained
from all sorts of interrelationship,
including sexual intercourse.'

'But reproduction as a consequence?'
'It depends...we have nine genders or sexes,
all very different.'
              'Nine?'
'Main ones. Also mutations, transformations,
 cultural rebellions, and joyful experiments, of course.'
Physically different sexes - nine?'
'At least. Mix and match, you call it here - anything goes.'

Don't you get confused?'
'With any luck!'

I FEEL LIKE DOING SOMETHING RECKLESS

Eyeing the tulips, plump as the point
at which we start to swell,
I thought the one who does not like to kill,
even to eat, might break gratuitously
some flower's neck,
                              trespass,
pluck one, squander the red blush underfoot.

Instead she chucked onto the wet street
a palmful of clutched coins.

I picked them up and keep them for her still.

Tulips flake like wallpaper,
flap about soft summer evenings,
when brute stamens suggest the past
or point at the impossible.

Two gather stalks on a lean beach...
...we share our indigence
like a contagious disease,
drunk with our own longings,
whose bodies pod dreams,
careless of where we are going,
so different, so amiable;

your thrown coins lie in a drawer in my desk,
long since unlooked at, yet
I remember how much you threw.

And I once flung, for a violent, a wild, wish,
a whole handful of silver
into a stream,

            from which, a winter later,
they recovered the body of a woman,
worn grey, no naiad, washed of her hurts,
a warning dredged from the water,
corpse-cold, hardened as putty;

her too I knew, bracelet-bandaged,
between lovers, hopeless, slashing her wrists,
finally embraced into this stiffened pose,
lax limbs, face without desire,
                              smile
watered down, softly put to sleep, unbelonging.

PINPOINT ANGELS

To number angels, feeling not the prick,
how many sit and settle on a pin,
nor sore of flesh of it, nor feeling sick,
then let me count and name them without sin,

touch all the parts of pleasure where they be,
sucking out stiffness, moistening the lips
and, calculating angles from the knee,
climb to the compound interest of the hips.

Those schoolmen angels, harbingers of hope,
converting England to a pontiff's dream;
such wanking of a fascinated Pope
allows me, centuries later, to blaspheme.

But still I sit and twiddle on this head
(with all those angels) on a needle's point,
disconsolate, for none will come to bed
how much they flutter, how much I anoint.

From all the labour I have of their wings
I ache (as they must) while the music drums,
and one of them interminably sings
which trembles all their bare, cherubic bums.

I cannot count them as they multiply,
rising unfettered, vague and numerous,
they dazzle as they flutter up to fly
out of my mind, away from intercourse,

like flesh-frustrating mermaids with no tongue,
abstract, diaphanous and lacking feet;
and, then, they seem peculiarly young,
all innocent, uncomplicated, sweet.

I have no saint to send to pagan land,
no crusty priest who waters with no flood,
no crispy wafer from the errant hand,
to soak the salty savour of Christ's blood.

Jesus - you have a beard yet woman's hair,
a face as sensitive as broken glass,
on pogo-prick you hover in the air
yet all these angels have a hairy arse,

and flap unfeathered wings, fresh with desire.
I count the knobs, an intellectual shrike:
eternal quiddity of hellish fire
will free us from the fixed point of this spike.

But I am stuck with fingering angel-souls,
invisible, accounted such and such,
aware in this of cavernous black holes
that tremble when I tentatively touch.

Angels dissolve like sugar when we stir,
they have a substance and a taste, are bright
upon the tongue;
                        the taste of him or her
until the darkness blinds us into light.

MASTER OF THE PASSIONATE UTTERANCE

There is a legend about China's most illustrious poet. It is the only recorded anecdote about him, and on it his reputation has rested for more than twenty centuries.

He had no desire to be known, indeed did everything to prevent it. Not even his name is known to us, let alone any of his verses. Yet he was accounted a prolific and passionate writer, a master of traditional forms who then invented his own, together with a doctrine or discipline of poetic patterning, the so called *Asymmetry of the Recurring Bias* - the plain, simple and euphonious three monosyllables of the original Chinese, as so often in translation, do not have that grandiose yet obscure ring which hangs about them when put into conceptual English. And as for German - his name there jars like a fork stuck in a dishwasher.

None of his work has survived; he did not let much of it see the light of day; what he did was to deposit fragments from time to time with this or that friend; or give impromptu recitals on the street at night to a companion or two, usually when a little inebriated. There would follow a wholesale burning of papers. References to it all have survived well enough, but no single line of any of his verses has come down to us by this method of distribution. Everything has been erased, even his name: he is always referred to as *the Asymmetrist of the Recurring Bias* - only the following story attests the basis of his reputation, and his other name: *Master of the Passionate Utterance*. How he came by the name is told in the following story:

The *Asymmetrist of the Recurring Bias* was reaching middle age, having devoted his life till then to the craft of putting feelings into words. He was dissatisfied and longed to discover the means to write a poem that would render it unnecessary ever to write another. As a pilgrim, therefore, he undertook the long and hazardous expedition to the border between India and China for an interview with the Grand-Master of Meaning, a man who spoke but once every ten years and then not much. Arriving at the monastery he found seven years were still to elapse. He applied himself to contrivances and experiments.

The time came for the audience. He read some of his verses aloud before the sage. The Master looked at him and said:

You command metaphor absolutely. You are master of the passionate utterance.

They stared at each other.

You must wipe from your diction every last trace of metaphor or simile, all figures of speech, all imaginary comparisons. In a word you must lose your tongue.

The poet gasped, in shock: *How must I convey the world's rich confusion and my own bewilderment?*

But time was up.

It is on the verse written after this dialogue that the poet's signal acclaim is founded. It is set out in full below:

PHOTOGRAPHS

Dead things, no living matter,
images imprinted on paper, firming the past -

yet ghosts slip and ooze
out of poses,
                    hover as smiles
incipient, also the traces
of how we became,
                    they show
as traits, and we recognise forbears
as descendants
                    will recognise us.

Memory is no different -
in preservation or cheating -

both are a chemical reaction
to various forms of stimulus,

photographs, and memory,
two ways of not being now,
prolonging the instant

into eternal recurrence?

How do we remember, and celebrate,
mourning ephemeral hours, but by

memory and
                    photographs?

BLEEDING

I am always bleeding, it seems,
the colour of blood is strong,
                              vivid, reminds
that we are living creatures:
                              trapped in tins,
my fingers; or my nose, now I am getting old,
for no reason stained hankies,
                    or the knife, on onions, slips
and the sharp stab, and I see my flesh
volatile and insurgent, open out, flowering,
you could say, though few blossoms are so bright,

unless roses.
                    So I can bleed! Means
I am not yet dead, but what losing

when these rouge petals are soon stopped
with the covering over of plaster,

and I no longer see the red efflorescence,

incandescdent, raging their lost
quiescence,
                    freely flowing,

panic and quietude, this is my blood,
not given to you, unwillingly shed,

breaking my body's defensive integrity,
telling me just how mortal
                              I have become,
and how thin, in all its sensitive doings,
how hollow, without redress, my skin.

PEANUTS

Peanuts?
           But was meant: penis? -
scouring the world's woes,
inserted or not.
           Hardened,
it is a warrior, ambassador
of our yearning, going into
dark places
           to look for solace
and release
           from strength;

and, weak, it is a stray thing,

dangling, soft, slender,

to be coaxed up into pride,
sucked dry of virtue,
unable to speak,

           though it sings,

upright and ready to spurt.

We have to trust
           such
unreliable appendages!

And would we not all be better,
taking into our mouths,
           dormant
and edible, redskin peanuts?

NO PLATES

Seeking a cafe, not Lake District, drab,
damp place, off the beaten track:
                                        I must
leave stock phrases, clichés we called
them once - that meant
unthought, not reaching
for right moments in words -

we found somwhere
                                to have a drink, cake,
served on slabs, wood or old slates.

You looked satirical, a tease or affront
to your neat table-setting:
                                Have they no plates?
and joked later, at home,
about having our soup on such -

but it was comforting:
                                happy
in how far we have come, together, gentle,
caring, no need to ask:
                                is this love?
Which we would not know how to answer,
but it is a familiarity, unspoken belonging...

do you know how much I have found you
a major concern
                                troubling my sleep
with strange dreams?

LAST JUDGMENT

resurrected
        shall we climb up
out of graves (what will
the cremated do: a magic breath
to recreate flesh from dust
                well
those phrases usually go the other way
                     so why not?)
     will it be
as absurd as living
            without strictures
trusting
     some
      the will of god
some
    the tough roots searching out
light
    the spreading
          of legs?
of care?
      the settled land
feeds cattle for us to consume -
              imagine
a sudden heaving up
          swollen earth
everywhere heaps of soil
          and all these people
no more weary or pale
        emerging
out of the ground
      to live again
         though not enough
angels to examine and sort through

TEACH YOURSELF CHINESE

trying to get over love
                        loss
                        liberation
new start follows dead end
but transition lingers longer
crossing over is hard
                        one method
was Chinese
                to learn from a book
it promised new life
                        things like classifiers
mixed up parts of speech
                        no tenses
away from the old embrace that turned bitter
grew cold
                I am not dead just numb
and the strange shapes and sounds
firing me up into a new world
where I unravel
                        unbecome
                                me
                                as sensation
leafing leaves left life
                        no principal parts
parsing out of the past
                        pre-sense
                                presence
present
        let me lift off and fly
                        far away
flickering like grass writing
out of chaos
                strokes
into meaning by pattern

Out of perplexity I have distilled
essence of loss, fragrant bewilderment,
mingled aromas -
                    wondering where you went,
what I've demolished, what I have to build,

what sounded out again, what questions drilled;
what I have cherished and to what extent,
pursuing always your peculiar scent,
found you,
            cornered, defeated, - so I killed.

We put you into earth and there you lay,
rotting for many years beyond our eyes,

your hair, your lips, your limbs were worn away,
as it must happen when a person dies;

silent, recumbent, settled you should stay:
so why, refusing rest, do you arise?

CHECKING THE FIGURES

Fabricateur; agent;
                         clerk of works: read,
think, peruse commercial letters, translate
into plain language, no nuance, just state
terms, price, conditions, delivery speed,
draft orders, file invoices, take no heed
of the way words dribble,
                              meet, congeal, spate,
tongue-thrust or lips licked, how will this abate,
downsettle to an emptying of need?

Columns to check,
                       ledgers to balance out -
for now I scribble verses on the side;
keep the lines neat, add up, there is no doubt

my figures show I have not falsified,
but all I ever wanted brought about?

A dream, of course, no wonder you deride.

TITLE OR FIRST LINE INDEX